IMPACT MANAGEMENT

IMPACT MANAGEMENT
Personal Power Strategies for Success

George J. Lumsden

amacom

A Division of American Management Associations

Library of Congress Cataloging in Publication Data

Lumsden, George J
  Impact management.

  Includes index.
  1. Executive ability.   2. Management.   I. Title.
  HF5500.2.L85   658.4   79-11632
  ISBN 0-8144-5519-0

First Printing

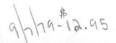

Acknowledgments

It is impossible to bring a manuscript from idea to reality without the help and understanding of a number of people. Here are a few who really helped:

Marge, my good wife, who suffered through the weekend chores by herself and missed a few enticing social events because I locked myself to the typewriter on those coveted off-days and evenings, and whose reading, chapter by chapter, was both constructive and supportive.

Jim and Nan, my son and daughter, who gave me the young person's insight into management impact; what they have seen—right and wrong—has lent perspective to my own views on the subject.

Edee Tyack, a true expert in taking the roughest kind of copy and turning it into readable text, who typed and proofed the material with a considerable sacrifice of her own time and patience.

Members of the National Society of Sales Training Executives who, in their semiannual meetings and their editorial submissions, have confirmed to me that what is written in this essay is relevant and useful in today's business scene.

And the staff of the Sales Training Department of Chrysler Corporation, who have suffered through some of my experiments and have survived, often teaching me more than I have taught them.

Contents

Introduction

My purpose in writing this book was to sift out for myself—and, I hope, for others—some of the reasons why managers are effective and why they are not. I have chosen the title *Impact Management* because I feel that effectiveness is measured not only by what a manager does but by how he does it. In other words, the manager's impact on his subordinates, peers, and superiors may advance or retard his ability to lead, achieve cooperation, gain recognition, and be promoted.

For practical purposes, let's define the manager as someone who is responsible for accomplishing work through a group of people who report to him and take direction from him. Such a manager should be in a position to initiate action, not merely to pass on instructions. I am speaking about managers, not line foremen who function principally as on-site intermediaries between management and workers. I also do not mean managers who are managers in name only—for instance, a sales manager who manages no one but himself and his own sales territory.

I will try to be objective. But I confess at the outset that this is not meant to be a learned dissertation. It is just an expression of the opinions I have formed after years of observation and reflection. My personal opinions have been tempered a little by those of others—people I respect who have points of view that differ from mine. Thus, what appears here probably is a reasonably representative composite of many opinions.

Let's pause for a moment to examine objectivity versus subjectivity. To be objective, we're told, is to be without bias or prejudice; to look at reality is to deal with facts. To me, the real world runs not so much on facts as it does on how people perceive facts.

When we talk about the impact one individual makes on another, perhaps objectivity is nothing more than accumulated subjectivity. In other words if you amass enough opinions, they become facts, or at least they pass for facts.

What I know of impact management comes from three different directions. One is the experience of being a manager in various environments at different times. Much of what I feel is true today has been true for a long time; conversely, a lot has changed. Another of my inputs is the experience of having worked for some exceptional managers whose examples have served me well. Still part of that same input is my association with several poor managers who have demonstrated the opposite. The third source is my experience in teaching managers, which required the study of experts and interchanges with students. Perhaps I should add a fourth influence: a value system established by my parents, polished by schools and churches, and confirmed by my wife, children, and friends.

The teacher in me won't let me stop at simply identifying impact factors. I'll splice in suggestions for behavior change and self-development as the book progresses. Perhaps that's the most important point I can make: how to cultivate good impact factors and get rid of the bad. It's important for all of us who are managers to keep learning how to be better managers, a thought that will be applauded by those who must suffer under our direction until we do.

At the end of many sections, there is an Interim Impact Inventory in the form of a brief quiz to test yourself on the management impact points that section stresses. Your answers—a *yes* shows impact potential, a *no* shows need for change—can serve as a guide to where you stand now and where to begin making improvements. The recognition of a shortcoming is often instruction enough for the person who really cares.

One last note. Masculine pronouns have generally been used when referring to managers purely as a typographical convenience. Good impact management is free of gender restrictions.

Part 1
Impact–What It Is and How It Affects Success

PUTTING IMPACT INTO PERSPECTIVE

Effectiveness. That's what we're looking for in a manager. My dictionary gives two solid definitions: adequacy to accomplish a purpose or produce desired results and capacity to create a vivid impression. We'll use both in discussing impact management.

Effectiveness is often confused with efficiency. Peter Drucker says that efficiency means doing things right, and that effectiveness means doing right things. I like that. In the long run, the effective manager sees to it that right things are done the right way.

In the minds of many, effectiveness means success. But that raises the need to define success. If it is limited to the few who rise to the very top of an organization, then I believe it is too restrictive. Many effective managers are denied that opportunity simply because the funnel gets pretty small at the top; as we squeeze up, somebody usually has to be squeezed out. Then, too, there are managers who find fulfillment in specialized fields and choose not to pursue higher positions. To the extent that they continue to be effective, they, too, can lay claim to success.

Although I would certainly label successful those who rise to the top, I wouldn't limit the label to the few who do. Success rises out of effectiveness. The label "success" can be applied honestly at any level a manager proves effective.

That prompts another point of view: my contention that those who enjoy the key leadership roles in any enterprise have, at one time or another, demonstrated their effectiveness. To be sure, there may be situations in which the Peter Principle applies (they may have risen above their capabilities); but as the dictionary explains, somewhere along the line they have shown an adequacy to perform, achieve results, or create a vivid impression.

Impact management requires that both performance and impression qualities be in place. This contention may trouble those who sincerely believe that performance is the only thing to be looked at. It may be nice to believe that performance *should* be the sole basis for evaluation, but it isn't! And that should send us packing to find out what else matters.

Two managers at lunch:

"I was surprised to see the notice this morning that Jackson was made vice president. What about Dingle and Peters?"

"They obviously thought Jackson could do the job."

"Well, that's probably true, but Dingle has a fantastic track record, and Peters has been in the field a lot longer. I worked with Jackson seven years ago, and he was okay, but he had a lot to learn."

"I don't know Jackson very well, but he always seemed to be a pretty decent guy."

"But he can't compare with Dingle—highest-volume territory in the country. It's not that I don't like Jackson, but I just don't understand how he made it over the other two."

"They liked him better."

Let's examine the above hypothetical conversation. If you've ever worked in a major corporation, you've heard and maybe even participated in one like it. It seems that this kind of reaction to management judgment is at least as frequent as "I'm glad Jackson got that promotion. He deserved it."

The person or persons who judge and promote managers, both present and potential, like to feel they are entirely objective in their decisions. They will argue that this or that person has proved himself in a smaller role and therefore deserves a chance at the larger one. Yet high producers are often overlooked in favor of *high impact* managers. That's because high impact managers couple *acceptable productivity* with *impressions of managerial quality* to make up a whole package. They make an *impact* on their bosses and, consequently, are given opportunities and help toward developing themselves for higher levels of responsibility. Indeed, they are often made into high producers and vindicate the initial judgment.

My experience in working for two major corporations—General Electric and Chrysler—as well as working as a consultant to other companies has let me observe this again and again. Take two candidates of similar background and potential for development. One is selected for advancement ahead of the other. There's no mystery in this; one had more impact than the other. Somewhere, somehow, there is a lesson here for the one who was passed over.

The same is true with the high impact manager and his subordinates. He may supervise people who are more technically capable than he, but he colors his relationships with impressions—impacts—that confirm his leadership role. Members of a work group are less likely to read production charts than they are to read and respond to the manager's personality, style of leadership, outlook on life, and general behavior in their presence. These areas of *impact* have a great deal to do with a manager's effectiveness in motivating people to make the effort required to achieve greater productivity.

In order that I don't give the impression that impact management is principally a matter of personality, let me emphasize that there are three basic impact areas:

1. The manager's knowledge and skill and his ability to apply them.
2. The manager's personal qualities and his ability to employ them.
3. The manager's attitudes toward work, people, and himself as revealed in his day-to-day behavior.

We are talking about the *whole person.* We are talking about *real situations.* We are talking about productivity and the *motivational forces* that bring them about. And we are talking about *effectiveness* and the outgrowth of it—*success.*

Most managers I know didn't set out to become managers. That's not to say they didn't aspire to higher and higher positions, but they didn't see management as a highly specialized bag of skills requiring special study and application. Rather, they saw management as recognition, privilege, freedom to exert themselves as individuals, and, not incidentally, as an opportunity to seize a healthier share of the good life. As in every motivational situation, the idea of what one gets outweighs the cost involved in the getting.

With the exception of recent college graduates, most of us grew into management, drifted into management, became managers as a matter of course, developed management skills on the job, and survived because good fortune exceeded our stupidity. (Recent college graduates have studied something about management, and they'll have to find different excuses for the mistakes they'll make.) Among older managers, the road to management generally followed the predictable path of knowing something, learning more, and trying hard. In many instances, succession to managerial status was not far removed from primitive modes of selecting tribal chiefs: lick 'em and lead 'em.

Again, many managers I know got into management as a result of their impact on those who had the power to bestow that right. Later, they had to exhibit impact on those who would in turn take direction. In some cases, the impact was largely know-how, genius, or merely mastery of the job. In other cases, it was an overwhelming arsenal of personal behavior characteristics that offset other deficiencies. In most cases, though, it was a combination of three things: knowledge and skill, personal qualities, and individual attitudes. These are what make them effective and their organizations productive.

The following section attempts to organize these into a usable package.

WHEN YOU WANT TO MEASURE, INVENT A YARDSTICK

Since I made the claim that a manager's effectiveness depends on what he knows, what he can do, and how he feels, thinks, and acts, I feel obliged to come up with a device to measure it. The yardstick I propose attempts to translate qualitative items into quantitative language. Because that is not too easily done, I'll confess at the outset that, for some, this yardstick will be only 30 inches long; for others, it will be 45. I am not as concerned with precise measurement as I am in establishing a format that allows the development of relationships. With that in mind, let's take the plunge.

The scorecard I've supplied lists three basic categories of management characteristics. Each characteristic is ascribed a *maximum* point credit. Under most categories there is an extra space for the reader to supply additional characteristics.

As you examine the chart, you'll note that the category labeled "The manager's knowledge and skill and his ability to apply them" has a maximum point assignment of 75. This means that, on the basis of a 100-point scale, a manager who is absolutely perfect in this area would be able to function at only 75 percent effectiveness. Just knowing the job is not good enough. It is not *impact* enough to make him effective.

What about the unfortunate manager who finds himself picking up only 50 points in this category? Can he manage effectively? To

Negative Impact Scale

Consider the following negative impact items. If they exist *in any degree*, subtract 3. If they exist to a greater degree, subtract 4 or 5.

Characteristics That Subtract from a Manager's Impact

Minus (3 *to* 5 *each*)

___ Arrogance	___ Uniqueness
___ Vindictiveness	___ Possessiveness
___ Recklessness	___ Unwillingness to take or share
___ Selfishness	blame
___ Laziness	___ Favoritism
___ Permissiveness	___ Isolationism
___ Abrasiveness	___ Lack of consideration
___ Intemperance	___ _____
___ Precipitousness	

Total plus score (positive scale)	_____
Total minus score (negative scale)	_____
Net management impact	_____

be sure he can. You and I have seen him do it. He makes up for his shortages by adding on points in the personal quality and attitudes categories.

Just as there's an upper limit to the impact a manager enjoys as a result of knowledge and skill, so there are limitations on what impact personality and style of management can contribute to a manager's effectiveness. In each category—personal qualities and attitudes—count a maximum of 30 points, for a total of 60 in the two. Does this mean that he can get by with only 40 points for knowledge and skill? On the surface, yes. But here is where the interrelationships between categories is important. If the manager just described truly has these fine qualities and attitudes, he will not allow himself to function at such a low level of knowledge and skills.

Another question: Are 100 points all we can assign? No, 100 is the impact level of the *acceptable* manager. A *really fine* manager could go to 110 or 120 points. An absolutely *perfect* manager (have you seen one lately?) could pick up all the marbles with 135 points.

Just for fun—and to validate the scoring system in your own

Positive Impact Scale

Measure yourself or another manager against the scale shown. Scores indicated are maximum. You may apply 0-maximum in any category. Total the score and log where indicated.

The Manager's Knowledge and Skill and His Ability to Apply Them
Plus (*up to*)

25 ___ Technical knowledge (basic understanding of the work to be done)

5 ___ Knowledge of organization (the system—how it works)

10 ___ Political sense (how to function within the system)

10 ___ Communications skills (ability to speak, listen, read, write)

20 ___ Organizing and planning skills (ability to conceptualize and assign work)

5 ___ General business knowledge (understanding of economics, accounting, marketing, legislation, etc.)

The Manager's Personal Qualities and His Ability to Employ Them
Plus (*up to 2 each*)

___ Physical attractiveness

___ Propriety of dress/grooming

___ Basic geniality/sociability

___ Vigor/endurance

___ Perceptiveness/awareness

___ Inquisitiveness

___ Thoroughness/orderliness

___ Decisiveness

___ Sense of perspective

___ Predictability

___ Patience/composure

___ Creativity

___ Integrity

___ Good memory

___ Optimism/sense of humor

___ _____

The Manager's Attitudes as Revealed in His Behavior
Plus (*up to 2 each*)

___ Self-confidence

___ Ambition

___ Determination/perseverance

___ Concern for quality standards

___ Concern for volume standards

___ Concern for profitability

___ Willingness to assume responsibility

___ Willingness to share credit

___ Willingness to take risks

___ Willingness to spend time/money

___ Willingness to take on unpleasant tasks

___ Objectivity

___ Fairness

___ Sense of loyalty/up or down

___ Concern for welfare/progress of others

___ _____

Total score (all categories)   _____

mind—run a rough rating on yourself or someone you know. See if a fairly cold appraisal approach is workable. We'll clarify and refine a little later on.

When you have finished scoring, turn the page. Here you'll find impact characteristics of a different sort—the negatives that subtract from effectiveness a great deal more than their positive counterparts add to it. Each of these negative characteristics has been ascribed a *minimum* value of 3 points and a *maximum* of 5.

Some of the negative factors may appear to be logical extensions of certain positive impact factors. They are. A good illustration might be the manager with a lot of self-confidence (add 2 points) who allows that self-confidence to become arrogance (subtract 5 points). Or the manager who is willing to take risks (add 2 points) but who then becomes reckless (subtract 3, 4, or 5 points, depending on the degree). Where we might admire a manager with ambition, that admiration can be offset by our dislike of his selfishness or self-seeking.

In every scoring system, we're confronted with the lack of exactness inherent in dealing with one person's opinion of another or the perception of another's quality or attitude, skill, or knowledge. It might strike the reader as odd that we would give a manager any points at all for, say, self-confidence, only to take points away for arrogance. Doesn't this mean that we're subtracting too little for arrogance, a quality most of us deplore? Look at it this way: A thoroughly deserving and self-confident manager who slips into an arrogant posture on occasion will lose a point for carrying a good quality too far. The person who is not all that self-confident but puts on a bad show of it—arrogance—gains little on the first score and loses much on the second.

The observer giveth and the observer taketh away—for reasons. On the plus side: 135 possible points. On the minus side: 75 possible points. Only a split personality could light up the "tilt" sign for us. We're talking about reasonably normal people in reasonably normal circumstances. In a test run of this scoring system with 40 managers I have known well, both in and out of my own company, the conclusions reached confirm the scale as being fair.

Effective managers are effective for a variety of reasons. Generally, it is because they are people who have both a knowledge of the field in which they work and reasonably well-practiced skills in handling assignments. They tend to be attractive in more ways than they are unattractive. They earn the right to power and they use it wisely. They build acceptance and respect among their subordinates, their peers, and their bosses.

These effective managers do not come to this point quickly—a thought that must be disturbing to some bright young people who, diploma in hand, are not suddenly moved into the executive suite. Effective managers wear in like the parts of an engine. Their initial impact may come from expertise in the business, or it may come from the simple fact that they have the title peers accept and to which subordinates respond. High initial impact may erode as the manager reveals certain personal qualities and attitudes, or it may build as he reveals others. Most of us have seen managers who began with good acceptance and ended without it. I can think of at least one person I worked under who grew in my admiration and respect. Time is important in the appraisal.

Perhaps this entire thesis is best summed up by saying that we look at managers in a *total* view. Whether consciously or unconsciously, we give points and take away points. When we say, "He's such a great manager in this respect that I can ignore that," the implied "but" means we haven't ignored it. It is true that there are plus qualities and minus qualities included in every appraisal, but the net result—impact—is the key to effectiveness.

If we can agree to that, perhaps the point count becomes less important. As was said earlier, our yardstick was developed to express relationships. If it does that, it has served its purpose. As we proceed, what is really important is continuing recognition of the great opportunity we have to change our own point counts as we come to see our strengths and weaknesses.

Part 2
How to Build Big Impact

BEHOLD THE EXPERT—HOW HE FAILS

Readers who place job mastery high on the credit side have, no doubt, been offended by the fact that I allowed only 25 points for technical knowledge. They will be further offended when I confess that I was going to give only 20 points to it until some of my colleagues talked me into being more liberal. You must admit, however, that of all the characteristics listed this one walked off with the biggest bundle.

Many years ago, it was my good fortune to be a counselor to aspiring young managers assigned to the Manufacturing Training Program of the General Electric Company. I call it a good fortune on two counts: first, in the 1950s a job at General Electric was like taking a course in management. Learning opportunities abounded, and the chance to observe professional managers in action was, to me, a revelation. Second, because I supervised the training effort at a plant location, I was in constant close contact with new hires—recent university graduates with considerable talent who were on their way to future management positions. I benefited from their recent education. More than that, I was privy to the evaluations their supervisors gave them, because we worked them out together.

Often, the least well received candidates were among the best candidates academically. The bright young engineer with a slide rule peeking out of his shirt pocket came with a lot of knowledge about electric motors—more than his boss had, one confided. But knowing about motors wasn't the objective. Getting them produced was what the job was about. When a trainee came to me one day with the objection that he didn't see much sense in taking some of the courses we offered because they weren't technical enough, I asked him what his job goals were. He told me he was an engineer and hoped to become a better one. I advised him that he was in the wrong program—the company had hired him thinking that he might become a manager. The courses he considered inconsequential were designed to help him function with an engineering background in a management role.

Management in that corporation had discovered that, though technical knowledge was important, it wasn't everything. Knowing how to design a product didn't necessarily get the product designed. Knowing how to make it didn't always get it made. The role of the manager was to harness technical knowledge to people who could use it in such a way that something came of it.

It may be misleading to use a highly technical company in this illustration. The same application could be made of the knowledgeable accountant's failing as a manager in an accounting milieu, or the artist's failing as the manager of an art studio. Perhaps the best example I can render from my immediate experience is the all-too-common failure of a good salesman who is plunged into a sales management role.

I recall an amusing old character who was a pretty fair toolmaker. He saw opportunity and opened his own business. Over the years, his little company grew steadily larger. He knew how to run every machine in his shop and enjoyed doing it. But as his enterprise grew, he found less and less time to put his hand to the work he enjoyed. Furthermore, as more personnel and machines were put under his roof and more money flowed into his cashbox, he encountered management problems.

He couldn't cope with it, so he invited his son to come in and run the company while he worked in the shop. The company president wore a shop apron, and the business flourished. My guess is that, if he had pretended otherwise, it would have foundered. Regardless of their specific knowledge of a job, some people are not capable of or are unwilling to take on management responsibility.

One of the great fallacies of management—and we seem to be escaping from it today—is that you must start at the bottom and work your way up. Knowing how to perform every job a manager supervises does have certain advantages, but not if that knowledge preoccupies the manager's time and thought. He may fall into the bad habit of doing rather than managing. Unlike the old toolmaker, however, he may not be smart enough to relinquish the management role.

Some years ago I worked under the direction of a very fine creative writer. He managed the editorial department of a successful sales promotion agency. His technical knowledge was one of the impact elements that brought him to management's attention, and he had been promoted on that basis. However, his image as a manager suffered because he continued to occupy much of his time doing the work rather than supervising others who were supposed to be doing it. Thus, his impact on those he supervised suffered.

My memory of that reasonably interesting but not very constructive experience serves me well in my own work. I head a department that develops and conducts training programs. I love both the writing and the teaching, and I do some of each. But I also recognize that my responsibility is to manage others as *they* do these things. When I multiply my technical knowledge by developing the skills of other members of the organization, more gets done than if I were to try to do it all myself.

Sometimes I feel that a little less perfectionism as regards technical knowledge may be of advantage to a manager. He is then not so likely to feel that, unless he does it, it isn't being done right, or unless it is done his way, it won't work. He is also less likely to boast of his own expertise. When a sales manager tells me he sells nearly as many units as any of his salesmen, I know he's not managing as he should. If he sells on occasion, that's understandable; a good manager should be able to fill in, take up slack, grab an oar, or man the pumps.

Placed in proper perspective, a manager's participation in the work has such advantages as a feel for what's going on, a recognition of problems, a means of setting an example, a demonstration of oneness with the work group. No more.

Another example: A promising manager in one sector of a business is brought in to take over a department with which he is reasonably unfamiliar. People gather at the water cooler to quiz one another: What does he know about this? What experience has he had? Whoever thought he'd be able to take this on? How long do you think he'll last? Has anyone set the date for the bankruptcy announcement? If that manager really is a manager, he makes the bridge in spite of his lack of technical knowledge.

To those who have said to me, "He'll have problems—he doesn't know the business," I have often replied, "Give me a true manager and he'll manage anything." There are flaws in that argument, but each of us knows at least one success story of a competent individual in a strange business environment who has managed well with a minimum of technical knowledge. Equal and opposite is the example of the technically qualified person who can't make a go of it because he lacks other attributes.

The effective manager who finds himself at a technical disadvantage will not be disadvantaged for very long. And it is interesting to watch how he goes about working off the deficiency. The first step is to discover what is *functionally* important. The second step is to discover who does what and whether or not there are any problems afoot. Then comes a series of consultations with key people for a refining of information. That eventually leads him to vital areas that require his own private study.

I have found myself technically disadvantaged a few times. In some instances, I coped well. In others, I muddled through. But even in those cases where I was obviously struggling, people were generous enough to help me see it through.

The most extreme example was my experience as a young naval officer during World War II. You could have folded my technical knowledge in a handkerchief. The blissful ignorance of youth kept me from being self-conscious until I learned a little about what the people I led already knew. (It was there I learned that the badge of authority was enough to get started; respect is earned as you go along. That, I discover, is still true in corporate life today.)

A lot of managerial impact comes from having the ability to demonstrate technical knowledge. Without question, this is the best single characteristic upon which to build managerial effectiveness. But it is just a foundation, not the whole structure. Any manager who doesn't have it must work diligently to acquire it, but the manager who has it, and not much else, will find the management road a tough one to travel.

Tennyson said, "Knowledge comes, but wisdom lingers." As we look at truly effective managers, we are pleased to see how they pursue knowledge rather than wait for it to come—and that makes wisdom hurry a trifle more. Knowledge may be vital, but the wisdom and skill to use it are what make the all-important impact.

Interim Impact Inventory

1. Were you specifically trained in the technology of the department you manage?

2. If you were not thoroughly familiar initially with the technical aspects of your department, have you since made a planned effort to overcome that deficiency?

3. Do you attempt to pass on as much expertise as possible to subordinates and encourage them in self-development?

4. Do you avoid doing the work of the operation, even if supervising others in their doing it means more time, effort, and frustration for you than when you do it yourself?

5. Are you quick to recognize the technical excellence of a subordinate, even when it exceeds your own?

6. Are you able to allow others to do the job their way (assuming the results are satisfactory), even though you might have done it differently yourself?

7. Do you recognize that your role as a manager demands more than just getting the work out?

8. Are you always looking for changes in technology, and are you willing to incorporate such changes into your operation?

"YOU GOTTA KNOW THE TERRITORY"

It's not what you know, but who you know. We've all heard that expression, and I'll confess to having said it—and meaning it!

What it usually refers to is favoritism. But in this case, let's look at the importance of the manager's knowing his way around the organization. This is vitally important in large companies, but it has considerable importance even in smaller ones.

In recent years, we have seen consciousness of organizational patterns emerge: This company sees that company operate with a certain structure, so they do some copying. In the automotive industry, there are striking likenesses, as well as a number of dissimilarities. This is also true in steel, electrical utilities, oil, and elsewhere. If it works for them, let's try it.

Divisions, departments, and functions within a corporate structure may look like their counterparts in other companies, but they may operate differently. Take personnel organizations, for instance. In some companies personnel people lead; in other companies they follow. In one corporation, the director of personnel may exercise considerable power in making recommendations and setting policies. In another, he may stand quietly by and wait for the word to come down and then dutifully keep records and defend policies.

One company tucks public relations under the wing of the advertising department, while another makes it an administrative function. In some companies training is a personnel responsibility, while in others it reports to the function for which training is performed. In my firm, for instance, our department reports to the marketing organization, although a few years ago it was a personnel activity.

Internal structure varies with different companies, depending on whether they're sales, financial, or manufacturing organizations. The internal climate of a company will favor one direction over another. I have seen sales organizations run roughshod over budget departments. I have also seen budget departments give fits to sales organizations. The program varies from place to place.

One reason why an effective manager in one part of a company can move to another part of it (thereby dropping back in technical knowledge) is that he knows the organization, the power structure, and the systems that will work for him. Such simple things as purchasing routines, expense account handling, or the copy list on memos are items we often rely upon secretaries to handle; but knowing them is still important.

In my first experience in a corporate environment, just after I joined the company, I recall the ease with which some of my new friends moved within their organizations while I stumbled over simple routines. I found myself doing things I didn't have to do and not doing some things that had to be done. As I began to find my way through the corporate maze it became easier. It didn't make much difference at that entry level, but at a higher management level it would have been harmful. In subsequent moves to other corporate organizations, I made it a point to study the road map more carefully.

Impact derives from knowing the internal workings of an organization in a number of ways. The manager who knows his way around demonstrates a sense of belonging. People who observe him see this as a level of self-assuredness, which is always a plus. They also see it as a command presence that says the organization was designed to help him get things done and not the other way around. He ties knots in the red tape but doesn't get wrapped up in it, saving time, trouble, embarrassment, and irritation. The manager is freed to do more important things and to be more pleasant when doing them.

Managers who move from one corporation to another would be

wise to accept the new system rather than try to change it. (Or, at least change it without fanfare!) I have seen managers come to Chrysler with preconceived notions that what was done at Ford or General Motors was better. Sometimes they were right. Just as often, they discovered that what worked over there just couldn't work here. In either case, those who made the most fuss got the least cooperation. Systems are a family affair.

In a related category, managers who understand the community environment and its power structures find themselves having more impact than those who don't. I have watched in wonder at the ineptness of newcomers to a plant location or a sales territory already established in the company's operations. Some consider their assignments a mandate to turn the community around. Some sulk and complain that this place isn't as progressive or congenial as the last place they were at. Some are handcuffed by local custom, particularly when it isn't accounted for in the company's policy and procedure manual. *The impact manager accommodates first, changes things later.* He knows that the territory can kill you if you don't stake out the swamps and thickets early in the game.

Jimmy Carter is a good example of a manager who suffered from not knowing the territory. He might have been better fortified for his initial struggles in the presidency had he served a term in the House or the Senate. It is interesting to note that, to the public's view, the going seemed easier in those areas where his close advisers knew the ropes. It probably was.

Roosevelt and Eisenhower were other recent presidents who did not have the advantage of congressional experience. But they had been close to the national picture in other ways and had contacts to rely on. Eisenhower's impact quotient as a war hero was high when he entered office, and that undoubtedly gave him running room to adjust. Roosevelt's first 100 days in office demonstrated how well he knew the system and how to work with it. Truman, Johnson, Kennedy, Nixon, and Ford all had contacts and close-up experience with the system; they moved with considerable ease and surety into the Oval Office.

Sizing up the organization and the community are important to a manager's success. That demonstrates wisdom. Getting the organization and the community on your side demonstrates power. And those are two impact elements worth cultivating!

Interim Impact Inventory

1. Are you thoroughly acquainted with the organization and the functions of the various segments of the organization in your company?

2. Are you careful not to bypass or preempt the authority of another department or function in the managing of your own?

3. Have you analyzed the power structure of your company and envisioned ways in which you can work with it advantageously?

4. Are you able to get to know—and have them know you—key individuals who can make your efforts more effective?

5. Can you adapt to the style or climate of the work organization or community until such time as you can bring about needed change with reasonable support?

6. Do you take the counsel of others in appraising the political climate and in the judgment of how to work within it?

7. Can you enlist the aid of others in gaining political support for your organization and your objectives?

"BUT I'M NOT RUNNING FOR OFFICE"

Playing politics may be as irritating to you as it is to me. I don't like it if it's contrived, manipulative, and self-seeking—as it is in a number of situations I've witnessed. But I do have to face one fact of business life: If a manager doesn't have political sense, he finds himself running from problem to problem.

At its worst, a lack of political sense can leave a manager friendless, impotent and, possibly, on the outside looking in. As someone has said, "The first rule of management is to stay employed." Although that idea may be a bit overplayed, it has some relevance. The objective of management is not to gather political support, but it is certainly simpler to fulfill management objectives with such support than without it.

Knowledge of the power structure is the obvious first step. Knowing *who* to deal with in that structure is the second. Knowing *how* to deal with that person is the third. Making it all come off naturally and positively is where impact is developed.

The impact manager generally deals as high up in an organization as he can. That's because the higher the approval, the more automatic the action all the way down. But think of the consequences of slighting some important individual in that hierarchy; you're likely to have footdragging or infighting of a subtle, undermining character that will make the project fail. Thus, impact managers don't always go to vice presidents. Sometimes they go just to managers who have ready access to vice presidents. The manager with political sense will recognize that power is often vested in someone a step or two below the top.

Finding the right person and knowing how to deal with a situation are often concurrent steps. Witness the following:

You're talking to No. 1, but are conscious of the power of No. 2. "Sam, I have a program that may involve your organization." (Explain briefly.) "You may not want to get into this at this particular time, but I want to clear it with you before I do anything further. Could we get together, or do you want me to handle the preliminaries with Bill?"

That's one way. Here's another:

You're talking to No. 2, who carries a lot of weight with No. 1. "Bill, I have a program coming up that may involve your organization." (Explain briefly.) "I know this is something you'd want to look at, and I'd appreciate your opinions on it. Is there any way we can get together to go over it? How about Sam [the big boss]? Would this be something he'd like to look at too?"

These are two very different approaches.

Now I'm thinking of two widely separated organizations within my own company. In one instance, I'd take approach No. 1. In the other, approach No. 2 would be correct.

The difference between one approach and the other is a matter of political sense. Good managers develop it. Effective managers use it. It affects relationships and accomplishments. It frequently makes the difference between winning and losing. Properly employed, it wins points for the manager—not only with the primary contact, but with others.

I work for a manager who possesses acute political judgment. I go to him with a problem that requires contact outside the department. I ask him: "Do you want to get in on this, or do you want me to handle it?" There's a primary political gesture even in that.

There may be a variety of responses:

1. "No, you go ahead with it. Just keep me informed about what's happening."

2. "Yes, I'll take care of it. I'll let you know how it works out."
3. "Let's both get in on it. I'll call Charlie and get the ball rolling."
4. "Let's both get in on it. Give Pete a ring and set up a meeting."
5. "Let me call Jeff and see what they want to do."

Getting the right people in touch with the right people is political sense. It doesn't mean just working through channels, although that's a part of it. It isn't simply a delegation of responsibility, although that's part of it too. It's getting to the action center through the action chain—without cutting out the wrong people or cutting in the wrong people. It's knowing whether to work from the top down or from the middle up. It's pulse taking of a very sensitive nature.

Political sense is being able to identify the bell cows and getting to them with your story before you lay it on the table for group judgment. For instance, in every group there are individuals who have adherents. If Jack says it's a good idea, it's a good idea. Then why not take your idea to Jack the day before the meeting and get his views on it? He may offer a few refinements that make it more acceptable to him. Or you may be able to change Jack's mind sufficiently in private so that he'll support you in public. That's political sense. That's what impact managers do.

Political sense has another cutting edge: It keeps you from becoming a political captive. Impact managers don't incur political debts, particularly those that may be hard to pay, such as, you do me a favor and I'll do one for you—which is generally a bad trade. (They'd rather have it the other way.) True impact managers generate a cooperative attitude that pays off all debts right now.

The effective manager employs political sense in still another way: in how he delegates responsibility. He doesn't assign Steve to contact Mac in another department if he knows that Mac doesn't hold Steve in high regard. He doesn't mismatch ranks if he can help it. He may send a grade 6 man over to get information from a grade 10 manager, but he'll send at least a grade 10 manager back to sell an idea.

Taking this idea back a step, notice how the politically wise manager selects people. Because he knows the importance of easy relationships, he hires people who show that capacity, and he hires them over the technically excellent ones.

Another evidence of political sense in a manager is the ability to time things properly—finding the right situation for introducing a project, for selling an idea. There are people who it is best to contact in the morning; some like afternoons better. There are those who like to talk things over at lunch and others to whom business talk at noon is unsavory. There are people who like a lot of advance notice, so they can give a decision after considerable thought. And there are others who won't make a decision unless they're at the eleventh hour.

I usually have a training program simmering on the back burner in some state of completion. It is the solution to a problem, but a problem not significant enough to merit much attention. It may never come to the fore; if it does, we can move forward. When the problem begs for solution, the time is politically right. That may be a bland expression of political sense, but good politics are seldom obvious.

The manager's concern is not only to effect impact up and across but to effect it down as well. Work groups are more amenable to directions at certain times than at others. With thought given to political effect as at least one guide, there is wisdom in sharing responsibilities. In that case, the concern of the effective manager is to bring about cooperation, not political maneuvering to pit one worker against the other. I've seen that kind of political strategy, but don't appreciate it, as either its generator or its victim.

It would be naive to leave off even a brief discussion of business politics without making reference to what I call the "party system," which tends to grow in direct proportion to the size of the company. Often, the leaders of the parties are not even conscious that it exists; but sometimes they are and encourage it.

The obvious advantage to the lower-level manager's identifying with an upper-level manager is that others will give way to him as a political expediency, simply as a matter of trading on clout. "He's one of Sam's boys, so don't fight him," is the kind of practical political advice often given, even if it may be the poorest business reason for doing something. It's unfortunate if that's all a manager is trading on. People and organizations can maneuver around such a person sometimes so effectively that the sponsor catches on.

The obvious disadvantage of power politics is that power is not eternal. Today's in-group may be out tomorrow. It is one thing to be loyal and supportive and quite another to be a satellite wholly dependent on a star. People at all levels can generally tell the difference. Political allegiances of the sort just described may be very effective on a short-term basis, but they can be quite hazardous in the long run.

We should give impact points to the manager whose political sense guides him through the maze of relationships he must cope with. The quality must be constructive before it can be labeled effective. And it has to play out in all directions, with all sectors of the power structure, before it deserves credit in the impact category.

Interim Impact Inventory

1. Do you attempt to meet and identify individuals with respect to their roles in an organization, even if there is no immediate cause to call on them for help?

2. Have you established a working relationship with key people who can help you achieve your work objectives?

3. Do you hire people and develop them with an eye to their political sense and acceptance?

4. Do you encourage your subordinates to work with others to enhance rather than jeopardize political relationships?

5. Do you and your subordinates deal with others open handedly so that they, in turn, will deal that way with you?

6. Have you cultivated senses of timing and priority that generate admiration and cooperation rather than rejection?

7. Are you careful not to become totally obligated or politically captive to any one person or group?

8. Are you aware that politics works down as well as up and laterally in both directions?

A SKILL YOU CAN'T AFFORD TO LACK

In my opinion, the highest impact managers are those with consistently high communication skills. However, this is not narrowly restricted to speaking skills. It is nearly as important to be able to listen, read, and write.

Speech skills build the greatest impact fastest. The late Charles Schwab once said that he would pay more for a man's ability to speak and express himself than for any other quality he might possess. To be able to express ideas in front of large groups ranks high in impact. Next is the ability to express ideas in smaller groups, interchanging points of view and winning approval from peers, superiors, and subordinates. It is probably because these skills are rated high that they are frequently key elements in management training programs. Unfortunately, most of the emphasis is placed on presentation skills and not on thought processes, which also count a lot.

The General Electric Company used to put all its managerial candidates through a course called Effective Presentation. At Chrysler, a similar program is offered, particularly to people in sales and marketing activities. In both companies, managers in prominent positions profit from their ability to handle speech assignments with reasonable ease. I have worked with a number of other major companies in agency relationships. Where attention to this skill development was evident, it always paid off. I have found that companies indifferent to speech skills often suffered because they were utterly dependent on an individual's own interest and ability.

A manager's platform presence has a lot to do with his acceptance. If he speaks with assurance, his ideas are usually felt to be worthy of consideration. The converse is true, too. It is unfortunate that some very fine ideas are rejected merely because the speaker is hesitant, inarticulate, or ill at ease. The Dale Carnegie program is not a favorite of mine, because it tends to ignore content and concentrates heavily on pep and personality. But I have to accept the fact that that's where the unknowing listener tunes in and turns on.

It is shortsighted to emphasize platform skills and ignore across-the-table speech skills that combine speaking and listening in a fifty-fifty balance. These skills play heavily on a manager's ability to raise the kinds of questions that get the other person involved. At the same time, they make points that win the case. In one-on-one and group situations, the manager who handles himself well does well. He *impacts.*

Managers not only attend meetings; they hold meetings. To run a meeting doesn't mean doing all the talking. Of course, the manager in the chair makes certain necessary announcements and explanations and controls interchange; but he functions best when he encourages participation. Thus, listening skills must be high on a manager's list. I recall with a great amount of admiration one manager who did this very well in groups and private conversations. He drew from others not only their points of view but agreement with his own. He was a master of the management-by-objectives technique long before anyone ever wrote about MBO.

Not so visible, but nonetheless important, are the skills of reading and writing. It was Francis Bacon who said that reading makes a full man and writing an exact man. A good manager needs to be both. The manager who reads (and how much there is for him to read today) keeps up on technology and maintains a sense of what's happening. Because he knows something, he has something to say. And he knows whether what he's listening to makes sense.

Because their horizons are widened by what they read, well-informed managers are more open to the ideas of their peers and subordinates and have more confidence in the directions their bosses give. Someone recently pointed out that fewer than 10 percent of the American public reads a book after graduation from high school. Well, you can tell which managers do and which don't! Whether they believe it or not, it has impact on those around them.

Although reading is frequently considered an elementary skill, there are some managers who read laboriously and haltingly. They would profit by a course in speed reading if it could be guaranteed that, by picking up speed, they wouldn't lose comprehension. I admire the manager who can pick up a report, scan it for total content, go back and read core items, and then decide what to do with it—all within a few minutes. Opposed to this are those who take the same report word by word; their mail processing undoubtedly takes an inordinate amount of their workday.

Writing is something else. I suppose I should be grateful for the lack of writing skill on the part of some executives, since I made my living for many years writing for them. In some cases it was their lack of skill. In others it was a lack of time. I could always tell the difference. A manager who knows how to write may not have the time to put together his own speeches, press releases, or announcements. In fact, his reliance on someone he trusts to do these things for him may be a real sign of his management skill of delegating time-consuming work. The difference lies in how this delegation is made.

In the case of the knowledgeable manager, there is always a prewriting conference, in which main ideas are set forth, with their order of priority and emphasis. There is an understanding of the audience to be reached and the objective to be achieved—both of which are helpful to the person working with him. In the draft review that follows, there is generally a moderate amount of fixing to be done, such as word changes and added emphasis. But it is done easily and quickly.

In the case of the manager who has no writing skills, there is an attitude of "put something together and let me see it." The teardown, postwriting conference is then a total frustration ("What I meant was . . ."). In most instances, it never comes off well, even if it's acceptable to the person for whom it was done. Garbage in, garbage out—as the computer people say.

My brother tells the story of an army captain who couldn't write even the simplest letter. Since my brother, a college graduate, was his clerk, the captain relied heavily on him for notices, reports, and other correspondence. When Roy's two years were up, his boss was profuse with thanks for his good service and said, "Type up a nice letter of commendation for yourself, and I'll sign it." Once in a while, I get a letter from a manager who has said something like that to his secretary.

This is not to say that managers should always do their own writing. I'm pleased when a member of my staff comes to me with a memo he feels should go out over my signature (political sense). It gets my signature if its purpose is proper and *if it is written well enough to represent me* to the intended reader. For a manager to allow writing to be less than representative is to lose a lot of impact.

Knowing *how* to communicate has a lot to do with the impact a manager makes. But knowing *when* and *what* is also important. My own work experience has been pleasant in that regard, because I have generally worked under and with communicators who have had good skills and sensitivity. They were managers of good conscience—willing to share information, squelch rumors, tell it like it is, and identify their own feelings along with it. These managers have built credibility and loyalty with their communications. They have helped people who work under their direction understand the problems and programs that affect them. The net result? Better performance—as regards both competence and motivation.

In evaluating impact as a result of communications skills, it's important to consider the entire spectrum. The lack of one skill may be greatly offset by an abundance of another skill. We've all known managers who aren't fancy public speakers but who are very fine counselors and conversationalists. Or managers who don't spend much time writing but who know a good piece of writing from a poor one. Some management jobs don't require an abundance of platform exposure. Some don't need a lot of writing support. Whatever the medium, whatever the circumstances, the judgment has to be made on the basis of adequacy and a sensitivity for communications needs.

One thing is certain: The competent communicator will always attract attention, get his point across, and reach his audience with a proper message at a proper time. That's impact that's easy to recognize.

Interim Impact Inventory

1. Do you honestly believe in the need for communication within the organization, and do you look for opportunities to communicate?

2. Are you reasonably self-assured and capable when making a presentation to an audience?

3. Are you often invited—and do you readily accept invitations—to speak before groups?

4. Are you a good participant in group meetings involving peers, superiors, and subordinates, and do you welcome such opportunities?

5. Can you chair a meeting without totally dominating it—listening and coordinating the exchange, as well as setting forth your own views?

6. Do you read beyond the mandatory paper-flow items that are part of your job?

7. Do you read with reasonable speed and comprehension; are you capable of identifying core issues and relevant facts?

8. Can you write a report or presentation complete from ideation and organization to final rendering?

9. Can you judge good writing from bad, and can you advise subordinates on how to improve their work?

10. Can you make sound judgments regarding when to use a particular medium with a specific audience, and can you perform in whatever medium you choose?

WHAT MANAGERS REALLY DO—SOMETIMES

The manager's ability to plan, organize, and delegate is very important to his effectiveness, yet there are many managers who don't do very much planning or organizing, and their delegation skills are pretty fragile. On the surface, one might feel that this is impossible, because that is the role of the manager. Let's consider a few cases.

Story one: John moves into an organization as manager. He has shown his capability to supervise people in a lesser capacity, so he is given a shot at the top job. On his first day in his new role, he recognizes that his predecessor had everything pretty well lined up. There is a workable system, and people are working within that system. He does the right thing and lets the system roll along.

Time moves along, circumstances change, and John's managerial task meets a few problems. He persists in doing things the way they have always been done, because he hasn't another plan to follow. His inability to cope with the new situation leads to his demise. That's one story.

Story two: John is a stimulator. He moves into his new assignment with zeal. People like him and respond to his leadership. His department shows immediate gains. Circumstances change, but John simply works harder, having no time to plan or reorganize. In the guise of a top-side manager, fate comes to his rescue. He is promoted before the department falls apart. His successor has to replan and reorganize before he can even begin to function and therefore looks bad by comparison. John, the culprit, is safely across town in his new office. He nods in agreement when others say to him, "That department hasn't been the same since you left it"—an illustration of the inequities of business life born more in ignorance than in malice.

I recall doing some informal counseling (mostly listening) with a very competent leader who had been put into a management job that required a lot of organizing before any action could take place.

His bosses had assumed two things: The organization was not in dire need of reconstruction, and the newly appointed manager was capable of doing what little organizing might need to be done. My friend was one of those people who, if you got the hoop rolling for him, would make that hoop roll better and faster than anyone else. But getting started was beyond him. He failed, and the company suffered losses in time and money.

It is possible for a manager, particularly in a highly systematized company, to function effectively without planning. Doing what has already been planned may keep him both busy and successful. Indeed, if he were to attempt to alter the plan, reorganize the function, or change its systems and procedures, he might logically be dismissed. This may be quite understandable in lower-level management roles. As managers move up in the hierarchy of leadership, however, sooner or later they are confronted with the necessity for planning and organizing skills.

The thoroughly competent manager will be able, even in a highly circumscribed management role, to ready plans and organization modifications that will be introduced as the need arises. These are the bases of proposals for improvement and form his defense if the present system falters. Even if there is no need for change in a given situation during his tenure, these thought processes and the planning practice will serve him well as he moves up the ladder.

Doers usually get more credit than planners. That's because doing is more obvious and planning is not so easily seen. But in the long run, managers who can plan and do are the ones who make it. It is a very insensitive top management that doesn't recognize this important factor of *impact*.

Maybe we've made planning appear ominous. It needn't be seen as extensive or even long range. Planning can be as simple as lining up tomorrow morning's work this afternoon. My best days on the job are those that end with a list of things to do the following day. (No, the best days are those on which I made the list the night before.) There are often items that get transferred from one daily list to the next for weeks on end. This is an understandable rearrangement of priorities. The fact that my notes stare me in the face each day keeps me from taking problems as they come. They're the basis of needed follow-up that might be forgotten, or they're the trigger for new projects that need doing.

Our department hasn't been reorganized in several years, but that doesn't mean we are operating precisely as we did since it was organized. Modest changes in assignments, priorities, methods, relationships, and reporting procedures have come about with changes in circumstance. A former employee coming back into the organization after a ten-year absence would have some difficulty in adjusting. These changes have been subtle and informal, but they have not been haphazard. Planning doesn't always mean submitting proposals and issuing new organization charts. It does mean thinking through and implementing to fit new needs.

Plans are made to be used. Organizations are made to provide manpower to implement plans. People are employed in organizations to follow plans and get things done. Yet how many managers are poor employers of available manpower? This is not to say there are people standing about idle, but that there are often people who are employed poorly, doing only a fraction of what they could do or doing work that should really be done by someone else.

More often than not, it's at this point that poor planning and organization skills on the part of the manager are first noticed—by the workers. If productivity doesn't match expectations, they then get noticed by top management. The word next gets around to other managers. It's an impact loss on every side.

There are a number of reasons why managers don't delegate well. One is that they don't have confidence in the abilities of others to do the work. (Training, please!) Another is that they don't like giving credit to people for doing things they feel lie exclusively in their own domain. Some fear that the worker will do the job better than the boss. Some don't know how to explain what has to be done. Some don't even know what has to be done. Another reason is that assignments fall into ruts (Max has always done that, let Max do it forever).

Some managers don't do a good job of assigning work because they're afraid to grant authority along with responsibility. Some don't like to assign certain tasks because they can put the workers in the spotlight. Some assign on a piecemeal basis: do this, and when it's done, let me know and I'll tell you what to do next. (A great way to develop Theory-X people is to make taskworkers feel as though they work for taskmasters.)

Impact managers like to plan meaningful work and give people a real chance to do it. They willingly delegate authority along with responsibility—once they're sure of the worker's competence. They make people accountable for a predetermined amount of productivity, are willing to compliment when the job is done well and criticize when it isn't. They're willing to cut across lines to give people new opportunities. They're willing to share in the workload themselves in times of pressure. They spread the burden if it is too heavy for one worker. Impact managers are effective in the Peter Drucker tradition; they do right things by getting the right people to do them right.

Proper employment of people is, in part, what McGregor talked about in Theory Y and what Herzberg meant in his comments about meaningful work. It's what Maslow was talking about, too, when discussing self-actualization. The proper assignment of work not only gets the job done, it gives the worker a sense of contribution and achievement. When workers feel their boss has given them such opportunities, they develop a sense of impact obtainable from no other source.

It's easy to recognize how important this skill is to management effectiveness when we face up to the truth that the sole reason for employing a manager is to get things done through others. If he doesn't multiply his own expertise through these workers, he isn't filling the assignment. The manager's planning and assigning skills are the pivotal point around which his whole job turns.

I'm a firm advocate of participative management—management by objectives, organization development, any system of management that gets people involved in goal setting and work distribution. None of these approaches allows a manager to abdicate his own planning and delegating. Indeed, he plans what others will plan, and he delegates planning participation. He designs the program in which others can function, and lays out work that others can do. It's perfectly possible to let others share in this, but only if the manager knows where he's going and how it's possible to get there. Little wonder we ascribe a high point score to organizing and planning skills!

When you see a manager who seems to know what he's doing and who knows what his organization is doing—and they're doing it—you are seeing a manager with real impact!

Interim Impact Inventory

1. Can you honestly say that your department functions under a specific plan—including objectives, target dates, quotas, and standards?

2. Are these objectives, target dates, quotas, and standards generally well understood and observed by all members of the organization?

3. Are the individual job assignments designed in such a way that, together, they can fully implement the overall plan?

4. Do individuals within the organization address themselves to their long-range assignments without a need for day-to-day instruction?

5. Are individuals within the organization participants in long-range planning and are their contributions to it identified and recognized?

6. Are you and your subordinates reasonably free from emergency or panic activities, and when such occasions do arise, can they be handled without undue disruption?

7. Do you replan your long-range activities completely each year, as opposed to merely updating or extending last year's plan?

8. Do the achievements or results in a given time period reflect the advance planning done for that period?

9. Are you consciously looking for new ways of doing things and new opportunities for productivity, and do you introduce such changes on a planned and orderly basis?

10. When you are away from your office for an extended time, are you comfortable in the knowledge that the work will go forward according to plan?

ON BEING WELL ROUNDED

We have all met individuals who are experts in their own fields but who are incapable of bridging to another. These are the people who start as engineers and end as engineers, who start as accountants and end there, who start as salesmen and think nothing else matters. While there is nothing wrong with that, these are not the materials of which chief executives are made.

As both an employee and an agency consultant in a number of corporate connections, I have seen many top managers function.

Top managers must be multifaceted because they have so many functions reporting to them. They have to see relationships between the market and the factory. They have to see what connection social changes have with worker attitudes. One minute they move in the world of exact science and the next in the milieu of public opinion. They are versed in what *The Wall Street Journal* had to say this morning, but they are equally well informed about how local athletic teams are doing.

These high impact managers understand a lot of things and are interested in a variety of activities, even if they don't have to work closely with them. They aren't experts, but they're reasonably well acquainted with things that touch on their own job even tangentially. That's because they know that what's happening way out there has significance for what's happening close in here.

I've known sales people who say, "Don't trouble me with all that bookkeeping stuff. That's for the green-eyeshade boys. Let them worry about counting beans, and I'll give them the beans to count." That's fine, Mr. Peddler, but you'll make a poor sales manager if you can't understand financial reports and economic factors.

Or what about the financial wizard who clings to his budgets and insists on strict expense control, ignoring a market opportunity that begs for some investment in advertising and sales promotion? Or the manufacturing man or the personnel manager or the anybody who gets so tied up in his own little world that he thinks that's all there is?

Impact managers are broader in their scope of understanding and appreciation than nonimpact managers. They are more interesting luncheon companions. They make better after-dinner speeches. They make better participants in conferences where solutions to interdepartmental problems have to be hammered out. They're better long-range planners, principally because they have a better perspective on today and how it relates to tomorrow.

I'm intrigued by the offerings currently being made by university extension departments and by organizations like American Management Associations, American Society for Training and Development, National Society of Sales Training Executives, (NSSTE) and others. To be sure, there are specialized courses offered, but also many general-information programs aimed at helping managers to acquire an added dimension. It is good for a manager to attend such programs and break out of a narrow field.

One of my most valuable associations is membership in the National Society of Sales Training Executives. At our semiannual meetings, we discuss our business—training. There is much talk about methodology and technique, but an equal measure of attention is paid to how a certain industry is facing its unique problems at the moment. As a result, I understand more about the pharmaceutical business, the steel, food, oil, gas, and electric utilities industries than I might otherwise have, and I'm richer for it. It helps me understand my own field, the automobile business, in a different way.

For instance, our NSSTE groups talked about the energy crisis long before it became meaningful to many others. Government intervention poses problems in our business, but it poses problems for others, as well. What people are thinking in Des Moines and New York and Albuquerque is important to business in Detroit. A manager can't afford to ignore or be uninterested in the world around him.

Reading—how much one does and what one reads—may be a good barometer of managerial impact. I'm impressed when I hear a financial executive discuss a current play or novel. It's particularly pleasing to me, of course, to hear a manager discuss intelligently some facet of psychology—not as an expert, perhaps, but as an interested party.

I recall one time when I found myself driving back to the headquarters city with the big boss—the really big boss. I knew him as a competent individual and as a no-nonsense manager, and that's probably what put me on edge. Visions of a four-hour conversation that would wring me out flashed before me. Dutifully, I brought up a business topic. Courteously, he responded—but not for long.

He searched out my interests and turned the conversation to my advantage. He bridged off into current happenings—not trivia but intelligent, meaningful topics. We hit on literature, the social sciences, geography, economics, politics, religion—all in an open, even exchange of information and points of view. The boss-man relationship was set aside in favor of explorations of mutual interest. Although I had viewed him before as a high impact individual, his impact rating with me soared even higher. And I may have risen some in his appraisal, too, because of my wholehearted and reasonably adequate participation.

A manager doesn't have to be totally informed on a topic in

order to participate in discussion; it may be enough merely to understand the vocabulary and a few basic ideas. But the more you accumulate in the way of general knowledge, the better position you are in to connect ideas and events to what you're doing in your own business.

Today technologies are so interrelated and communications are so rapid that a lot of general information is dumped on our doorstep. Chrysler's involvement in the space industry gave it early access to materials and devices that made their way into automobiles. The electronic ignition system and the lean-burn system, along with striking improvements in radios and other automotive appliances, were brought along faster because of this interface with a nonautomotive division. The same is true with an individual manager who moves out beyond the narrow confines of his own department or his own company; he fits new ideas to old ones, thereby improving his operation.

Breadth of knowledge does several things for a manager. It lets him see relationships in current events that may have meaning in his own business. It lets him see what others have done that could benefit something he's doing. It gives him insight into other people's ways of doing things. It prepares him at a lower management level to move comfortably to a higher one. It helps him relate in a more intelligent manner to people on his own level and with those who work under his direction. It takes him away from his workbench and into the world long enough to get a better perspective of who he is and what he's doing.

Most of all, it makes a manager a more interesting person. He can connect with more people and more situations than the narrow-gauged person. That's the kind of impact that allows him to function more effectively.

Interim Impact Inventory

1. Do you seek opportunities to attend conferences and seminars that might broaden your views and put you in contact with business people other than those in your own company?

2. Do you read beyond the normal across-the-desk materials, such as books and periodicals and the like, in an effort to understand wider business and social concepts?

3. Even though you may not enjoy it, do you expose yourself to enough radio, TV, and current light literature to know what others are talking about?

4. Do you break away from time to time to attend a concert, a play, an athletic event, or a speech by someone not associated with your business?

5. Do you make it a point to have lunch on occasion with managers in other departments and in other companies?

6. Are you involved in some outside activity (a service club, church or synagogue, fraternal organization, or professional society) where topics other than your own business are discussed?

7. Can you enjoy yourself listening to and participating in discussions that have nothing specifically to do with your business?

8. Have you ever taken a course or read a book with the specific objective of learning more about a part of your business that affects you only indirectly?

9. Do you encourage others, as well as yourself, to broaden their interests and contribute new thoughts to the function of your department?

Part 3
Personal Qualities
That Add to Impact

TAKING A PEEK AROUND THE CORNER

What we've looked at until now are the heavyweight aspects of a manager's bag of knowledge and skills. These are what the job is all about. Without these skills and knowhow in fair measure, managers can't function. In fact, people who can't demonstrate potential in these areas are not likely to be given the opportunity to manage.

Forty years ago, when I first went to work, a competency and interest in job-related skills would pretty much have satisfied managerial needs. If one had a job back in the Depression, who cared what kind of person was boss of the gang? The boss was *numero uno*, the biggest or the smartest, sometimes both. You respected the position if you didn't respect the person. In those days, a worker's hope was to stick with it long enough to outlast the miserable so-and-so and maybe work up to the top job himself. It was a workable, if primitive, motivational concept.

This management posture did not exist because managers didn't care what workers thought; they simply didn't think it made any difference. Everyone came into management under older managers who thought just as they did. Get the job done was what they were all told, so they did it. They weren't necessarily mean, but they didn't feel obligated to be particularly polite. Nor did they see any particular reason to be constructive. With many managers, the idea was to cut jobs down to the simplest level. If you couldn't do it, tough.

My first real confrontation with this point of view came when I was a stock boy and bag-packer at one of the first A&P supermarkets (a pretty primitive affair compared to today's A&P stores). The manager was a decent man, all business, but decent. The assistant manager was an odd person who saw his function as the operational spy. His motivational approach was: "I'll tell on you!"

The area supervisor was the heavy. When he was in the store, he bossed the stock boys, the butchers, the cashiers, and the manager. Maybe that's why we liked the manager; we felt sorry for him. Mr. Big didn't care if you came up with a hernia. He almost said as much. He just wanted you to carry more boxes faster.

My hours of work were from 3 to 6 P.M. on schooldays, 7 A.M. to 10 P.M. Saturdays. One weekday afternoon I arrived at the store 15 minutes early and was sitting in the basement waiting for the appointed hour. A typical teenager, I was always hungry, so I had dug into a box of cookies from the breakage bin—merchandise that had become unsalable. Mr. Big rolled into the basement at that point, spotted me, and told me to get to work. He accused me of stealing from the inventory. It was a big scene. No explanation would do. I did what seemed smartest: I went to work ten minutes early. That won me no prizes, either. In subsequent months, when Mr. Big was around that store, I took my share of shoves, bumps, sarcastic remarks, and floor-sweeping assignments (after hours, at no pay).

I tell this quaint tale not to evoke compassion for my blighted childhood but to illustrate a point. There were about 12 part-timers like myself, all equally against Mr. Big. And we found ways to make his job difficult. When he asked for a particular item, it took longer to find, or we hid it so that he couldn't find it. When it was known that he was looking for someone to do one of his special assignments, we hid. It's amazing how many of us had to go to the bathroom all at the same time. He was such an egotist that I don't think he realized we had our own ways of fighting him.

Although he was a tyrant on breakage, he was, nonetheless, a willing participant in consuming it. Salted peanuts in cellophane bags were always breaking (navy beans, rice, and barley, packed in the same bags, never seemed to have that problem). Mr. Big—all 300 pounds of him—would nibble away covertly at our peanut supply. Word passed among us on a certain Saturday afternoon not to eat any of the peanuts. We learned, somewhat after Mr. Big did at first hand, that a few garlic buds had been carefully chopped up and stirred into the peanuts. We had learned not only how to make his job difficult but how to make his life miserable.

Twelve scrubby teenagers in their soiled white shirts and black bowties, working for two bits an hour in a down job market, dared do that. They took a boss who, without question, knew his business and had probably earned the right to supervise, and leveled him. They withdrew their permission to be managed. We were not delinquents, because we worked hard and cooperatively for a manager we liked. But we minimized the effectiveness of the intruder we didn't like. If that kind of silent rebellion could happen in those times, think of how it happens in these less respectful days!

There are still a few Mr. Bigs and a few Captain Queegs afoot. They may not be as obvious, and sometimes they try to disguise their real qualities with a patent-leather niceness. When they do, we have to concede them points for trying. People respond to the bull-of-the-woods type of boss with enough foot dragging to minimize effectiveness. On the other hand, if we can add impact with constructive personal qualities and attitudes, that manager's effectiveness will flourish! It's an industrial version of the foundation stone of American democracy: those who rule do so with the consent of the governed. And let's add another important dimension—with the support and cooperation of the governed.

The personal qualities and attitudes revealed in behavior are important factors in a manager's impact. This is true in upward and lateral as well as downward relationships. We're looking for reaction, so it's worth considering the actions that bring about good reaction.

As we proceed with discussion of plus and minus qualities, we should see them not so much as efforts to produce nice people but as what is needed to produce effective managers. Of course, the byproduct of making them nice would be all to the good. The qualities we will be discussing are those that bring about such things as respect, admiration, confidence, and trust. We may not always like a manager, but we can have trouble arguing our dislike for him. Good qualities may, indeed, work against a particular point of view and engender momentary dislike: but on balance, they are still good qualities. Take integrity as a quick example: One man's integrity might cause another's embarrassment.

We often find ourselves thinking, if not saying, "He's just naturally a decent person. Patience is his middle name. Decisions come easy to him. Friendliness is part of his nature." True, many of us were brought up in environments that make these qualities appear to be natural. But that's not always the case. We were taught these qualities. Our behavior was learned, sometimes by following a nearby model, but more often by careful study and analysis followed by practice. We should really think of these desirable qualities as skills, regardless of whether they seem to be natural or developed.

As we probe into these skill areas, then, let's consider how we can add them to our own toolkit, and put them to use in our own jobs. In many instances, the going may be rough because I'll be describing skills I have yet to develop for myself. (Each of the personal quality and attitude skills will be covered in the same order as they appear on the scorecard. Their sequence has nothing to do with importance; it is just a matter of convenience.)

WHAT YOU DO WITH WHAT YOU SEE IS WHAT YOU GET

Initial impact is nearly always visual. Long before we know what kind of individuals we're dealing with, we see them and form opinions. If what we see is pleasing to us, we look for other good qualities. If it's not pleasing, we tend to hunt for other poor qualities to support our first judgment. The old cliché "You never get a second chance to make a good first impression" has truth in it.

We're emotional creatures. Although we pride ourselves on being logical, logic generally comes into play only after emotion has established its beachhead. I think it was Charles Dickens who, when asked how he felt about a certain person, said he didn't like him. Asked how well he knew him, the response was that he didn't know him at all. Then, as an afterthought, he added: And I don't want to know him, because if I did, I might like him.

People look at the package before they buy the merchandise. They look at the styling of an automobile before they explore its driving and riding qualities. That's true, too, with managers. We size them up visually before we evaluate them as people. I may not necessarily think that's good, but it's a fact of life. Even after a relationship is established, the day-to-day visual impact has a plus or minus effect. I have known people to quit jobs simply because they couldn't stand to look at their bosses anymore.

This is not to say that God ordained some to succeed and others to fail because of the slope of one person's shoulders or the shape of another's nose. What we have is what we have, but what we do with it is another thing. I have seen some not-too-handsome men and women who became physically attractive because they worked at overcoming their natural states. Conversely, some basically attractive people let themselves drift into becoming pretty dowdy specimens. We'll discuss physical attractiveness and propriety of dress and grooming together because they're like salt and pepper—different, but well paired.

These impact areas may have importance all the way back to the interview that puts the manager into a job. Give me a well-proportioned and well-groomed applicant, and I'm inclined to look at the other qualifications favorably. I have probably passed over several geniuses because they presented themselves poorly. The canard about the interviewer who, after screening a dozen applicants, picked the good-looking blonde with the fantastic figure isn't entirely a joke.

The same is true in considering promotability. My own observations reveal there are more promotions among the physically attractive and well groomed than among those who are not. I would call this the most flagrant sort of discrimination if it were not for the fact that those who were rejected could have done something about it.

The Bible says that no man, by giving thought to it, can add one cubit to his stature. That may be one of the few passages of scripture that hasn't been debated to death. But that admonition doesn't preclude our doing the best with what we have. It doesn't advise against buying suits that fit. Tailoring and fabrics can add to the impression of height if shortness is a problem; or they can add to the impression of breadth if extreme height is a detraction. Nor does it say it's futile to get the right kind of hairstyle or suitably shaped glasses, to grow a mustache or shave it off, to stand and sit and walk with good posture, or to take off those extra pounds that make last year's suits fit badly. It's not necessary to be ravishing to look attractive.

The higher the management job, the more sensitive this impact area becomes. Managers become representatives of their companies. And they become representatives of their bosses. I'm pleased to be surrounded by people who care enough about themselves and their company to keep fit and dress carefully as they conduct training conferences about the country.

Why all this fuss about physical attractiveness? Well, for openers, it shows people you care, both about yourself and about those around you. Sure, there are slobs in management roles who are very effective despite their slovenly appearances. Think of how much more effective they might be if they showed more care about the impact of the way they look.

Business operations take their signals from managers in a variety of ways. Impacts, as we've noted, are impressions received from what is seen, heard, and felt. The impressions may be quite erroneous, but they are there. A simple example: I take my car into a dealership service department for repair and am met by an unkempt service manager. He turns my car over to a sloppy-looking mechanic. My automatic reaction is, "I hope they know how to do it right." This is not unlike the reaction to a physically unattractive manager.

A few words about propriety in dress and grooming are now in order. This means not only dressing and grooming to enhance the physical self, but doing so in sync with the environment. We don't wear white tie and tails to the beach, nor do we wear sandals and a Hawaiian shirt to a big dinner at a hotel ballroom. Just as clothes should fit the person, so they should fit the occasion.

Managers should be rather circumspect about the company's dress code, whether that code is implied or expressed. The code is what is done, and it doesn't take long to recognize it. There are conservative companies and liberal companies, and there are companies that don't care. In no case, however, should a manager not care, because a lot of important impact is lost by doing so.

Some years ago, I worked for an agency that did a lot of work for General Motors. My habit was always to wear a reasonably conservative business suit to work, and I felt quite at home during my frequent conferences with executives at the General Motors Building. One day, I had lunch alone and was walking in the vicinity of that old landmark with time to kill, so I decided to shop for suits. I walked into a nearby store and was poking around some racks when a salesman approached me.

The suits I was looking at were even more conservative than any I had in mind—dim stripes, solids, imperceptible checks, all tailored modestly. I said to the clerk that these were not my style; did he have others? His reply was, "You don't work for the Corporation, I take it." He took me to a part of the store where a wider assortment was available. Shades of my old Navy days when, if you wanted to buy a uniform, you bought it near the naval base. To my knowledge, that corporation doesn't have a prescribed dress code, but its more impact-conscious executives had adopted one.

At Chrysler, one very effective manager I know tells his subordinates that he has no objection to their wearing sport jackets, so long as the pants match the coat. He laughs. They laugh. He wears good-looking, complete suits. They wear similar complete suits. He has a very nice-looking department.

After an extended absence from the home office, another of our managers came to a meeting sporting a longish hairstyle. At noon, he skipped lunch and found a barber who trimmed it to a more conventional length. His own sense of being with it (or remarks passed by others) made him do so. The point is that managers who want to fit into an organization can't be square pegs in round holes.

We went through a period in the early 1970s where anything went with anything, and to me it looked gruesome. I feel that, if you wear a paisley tie with a striped shirt under a plaid jacket, you fit the mixed-up outside world we live in. Yet perceptive managers at our company and in other companies all over town stayed away from such crazyquilt costumes. So, too, did the outstanding training managers I met at meetings of the National Society of Sales Training Executives. Flashy sport jackets came out at informal gatherings, but they were left in the closet when the impact-minded manager went to the office.

Expert observers have noted that successful executives are conservative dressers. Are they successful because they are conservative, or conservative because they are successful? Who cares? Dress with discretion, and you minimize the risks of being wrong.

Of course, there are management jobs that aren't suit-and-tie occupations. In such cases, maybe the boss's appearing in a hard hat and work boots is how it is and where it's at. Still, the better he wears those items, the more impact he has.

In spite of the populist trends in present society, people still like a manager to look the part. They respect people who respect themselves and their positions. When you consider that the effective manager is one who gets others working on his behalf, then it's not unreasonable to expect that he'll get a tailor, a barber, a laundry, and dry cleaner to work effectively for him too.

There are some who would contend that the interest expressed here in dress and grooming is extraneous to the true effectiveness of a manager. They would charge that this is superficial and that judgments of this sort are wholly subjective. Well, impact does deal with the superficial in a most annoying way, and subjectivity is baked right into it. Opinion is strongly, if quietly, on the side of a quiet appearance, neat clothing, and good grooming. This accumulated opinion is a fact of business life, and we live with it.

Interim Impact Inventory

1. Do you routinely groom yourself each day so that you could play host to the president of the company without discomfort or embarrassment?

2. Are you inclined to check the neatness of your grooming from time to time throughout the day?

3. Do you attempt to keep yourself in reasonably good trim so that your overall appearance suggests you care about yourself?

4. Are you careful when selecting your wardrobe to choose clothing that allows you to dress to fit the occasion?

5. Do you seek the advice of people whose taste you admire and trust when it comes to selecting the styles, colors, and patterns of your outfits?

6. Are you likely to discard items of apparel that, although not worn out, have gone out of style?

7. Do you pay attention to your standing, sitting, and walking posture to present yourself properly at all times?

8. Do the people in your department follow your lead in dress and grooming habits, and do they represent you well?

TWO MIRRORLIKE QUALITIES

There are two other qualities easily dealt with together: geniality or sociability and vigor or endurance. What's particularly interesting about these qualities is that they are like mirrors—demonstrate them, and people respond accordingly.

There are managers who don't understand this. For them, greeting people with a cheery "Good morning" is a waste of time. They nod and grunt merely to acknowledge that they know you're there. If they do offer a greeting, it's done with apparent reluctance. It isn't long before the staff returns greetings with the same feeling.

I have seldom found effective managers to allow themselves to become bound by ties of friendship with subordinates. This is not what I am talking about here. Popularity is not at issue; approachability is. We're talking about exchanges of warmth, transactions that imply respect, consideration, and humanity. Walk into an office charged with coldness due to inconsiderate internal relationships, and you'll seldom encounter warm feelings for outsiders. Some stores are run that way. Some corporate departments are run that way. When they are, people from the outside don't want to transact business there.

Cold internal relationships close the doors between bosses and workers. I recall an incident in one company where an untenable condition had developed, and nothing was done about it. I asked one of the people why he didn't let Bill, the boss, know. I was told that the only time you talked to Bill was when you had official business to transact with him. My comment was that it seemed that this situation sounded like official business. "Yes," came the reply. "But if I tell him about it, he'll automatically think I caused it." Cold, unapproachable, and bypassed.

I worked for a manager many years ago who was unsociable with his employees but put on a hail-fellow façade in front of others. Employees who witnessed this were even more annoyed. If you're going to fake it, fake it 360 degrees. Otherwise, it won't wash.

Sociability has its limits too. I always appreciate some manager dropping into my office to pass the time of day, but I'm not pleased when he passes the entire day. I have a rule of thumb on that: If you're going to do business, take off your coat and hat and sit down. If you're not, stand in the doorway—but not forever.

Then there's the manager who thinks he's making impact points by regularly going out drinking with the guys. That's fine, but not as a routine. He should know that he has to leave the work gang long enough so that they can talk about him once in a while.

Managers who encourage openness in their operations do so by first being open themselves. They display friendliness and respond with it. They wear a smile and say "Hello" when walking through an area. They get into the habit of using names. They initiate a conversation about workers' families, vacations, or physical well-being. They don't pry or press themselves into the company of others except by invitation.

I have known managers who choose not to encourage sociability, because they say it not only wastes time but gives others the feeling that wasting time is acceptable. There are two parts to that: (1) It doesn't waste time if you consider it an investment in producing effective relationships. (2) It doesn't encourage time wasting if the manager keeps the session within specific time limits. Using and abusing are two different things.

Getting to know people and getting them to know you are important in easing business transactions. If it isn't a natural quality, it can be developed. Indeed, it has to be developed for optimum impact.

A manager's health may affect performance. It can have much to do with relationships with peers, superiors, and subordinates. I recall one former associate who was deeply concerned about his own health, and he brooded about it. In the company of others he took a very quiet, uncommunicative posture. His preoccupation with himself was interpreted by others as indifference or even opposition. When his health took a turn for the better, so did his personality. He reacted better toward others, and they reacted better toward him.

The race may not always be to the swift and the battle may not always be to the strong, but my observations of managerial winners lead me to put my money on those who have vigor and endurance. Somehow, the 40-hour week has escaped me. The *effective* managers I know spend a great deal of time doing their jobs, even if they do not spend all that time at their desks. Management jobs may be largely mental, but they are also physically exhausting.

There are two things that require discussion here: The *real* vitality of the individual and his expressed vitality. If you're not healthy, the best advice is to see a doctor and start going in the right direction. If you are healthy, then it's important to act healthy, move with alertness, and keep going. Most dynamic corporations today don't give managers a lot of time to rest, and they certainly don't pass out prizes for shuffling along.

We expect vigor and endurance in younger people. We are impressed with it in older people. So the older a manager gets, the more conscious he has to be of it. Not acting with vigor is often interpreted as acting without zeal. The training staff where I work has an average age of over 50, and it demonstrates daily to younger managers and salesmen that it's not a young person's world until the old-timers give it up!

The old cliché that says "The speed of the boss is the speed of the gang," makes sense to me. The vigor displayed by a manager filters down through an organization. But it has to be vigor within the capabilities of the people being led, and endurance expectations can't be excessive. I have known of offices where nobody dared leave in the evening until the boss left, which is ridiculous.

Managers should not expect employees to mimic them in their every move. But senses of commitment and moving forward aggressively and alertly are worth displaying.

Sociability opens the communication process without which management cannot function. Vigor and endurance set a pace that generates excitement and results in productivity. And management can't function without them!

Interim Impact Inventory

1. Are you generally warm in your relationships with people or capable of acting so even if you do not always feel up to it?

2. Would you say that people nearly always feel comfortable in your presence and that you exert an effort to make them feel that way?

3. Do superiors, peers, and subordinates seek you out for informal chats or for your company in social settings?

4. Can you control interoffice social visits in such a way that wasting time is minimized while, at the same time, you maintain a level of geniality?

5. Have you had a physical checkup lately, and do you act as healthy as your doctor says you are?

6. Do you move as though you're busy and interested and eager, and by doing so, do you set a good example for others?

7. Do you take a vacation from time to time to recharge your business batteries?

8. Do you act, think, and express yourself as though you're on your way up as opposed to on your way out?

SENSE AND SENSITIVITY

George Odiorne, the articulate exponent of management by objectives (MBO), says there are some managers who make things happen, some who watch things happen, and some who don't know what's happening. Of all the indictments a manager should avoid, the last is the most important. He should keep eyes and ears open and his head on a 360-degree swivel. What he can't see and hear, he should be asking about.

Perceptiveness or awareness is (or should be) followed closely by inquisitiveness, and we'll pair them in this discussion.

Awareness of what? Smart, effective managers know that their work is done with information that must be translated into action. They therefore require reports on such things as productivity, revenue, costs, absenteeism, the condition of facilities and equipment, and market trends. Any condition that impinges on their operation is something important to their success. They have to know before they can do anything to maintain satisfactory operations or improve unsatisfactory ones.

But there are other bits of information that never appear in reports. Sometimes a manager has to resort to the old Indian skill of putting an ear to the ground to hear what's happening beyond the line of sight or normal range of hearing. Feelings, for instance. How do people feel about what's happening? Are workers tackling their jobs with enthusiasm or with reluctance? Is a certain policy being adhered to or just winked at? Are there certain gut feelings being kicked about in the marketplace that could have an effect on next month's sales?

Knowing more than people tell you is important to a manager. Key managers in the Nixon administration knew that. Their preoccupation with that idea led them to excesses. The irony of that situation was that they, in turn, backed into a position of concealment.

What we're talking about is a thousand miles away from wiretapping and bugging or any other covert peeking over shoulders. Alert managers read feelings in the eyes of people with whom they hold routine conversations. They read reactions in the faces of people to whom they give orders. They listen to how things are said, noting the subtle overtones in conversations.

Even more alert managers let people know in advance that they are interested in being informed, that valid information existing only in opinion is also welcome. They follow their own seeing and hearing with questions that encourage offers of more information. Interestingly, people often withhold information because they don't think the boss wants to be bothered. Sometimes it isn't because they don't want the boss to know, but because they don't think he cares to know.

One reason for my enthusiasm for participative management styles is that a free flow comes out of any style that encourages the exchange of information. Do-it-yourself managers can't be bothered to conduct meetings for the exploration of points of view. Neither can they be bothered by the information they don't have. Managers who operate in the dark don't usually make it.

There's a side benefit to a manager's perceptiveness and inquisitiveness. People who see that a manager cares about information see a manager who cares about the department, about what it's doing, and about the people in that department who are doing it. It's an impression, an impact, that's important, because they then respond in kind.

Managers have to go below the suface. They have to be perceptive, aware, and inquisitive. The key word in management is probably "decision," and decisions are best made with a maximum of available information. Decisions also have to be made to isolate the correct problem. Interestingly, some management action is misdirected and treats symptoms rather than causes.

The impact factors of awareness and inquisitiveness have two sides: (1) the effect on subordinates and associates who recognize that the manager is on top of things and in on things and (2) the effect on the manager's own ability to see problems and find solutions for them. Managers should develop perception and inquisitiveness for both reasons.

Interim Impact Inventory

1. Have you developed a skill for seeing without spying and hearing without eavesdropping, and are you capable of knowing what's going on?

2. Are you seldom surprised when a subordinate reports an out-of-line condition to you?

3. Do you require subordinates to report to you formally and on a stated-time basis, so that routine information flows routinely?

4. Can and do your subordinates voluntarily call your attention to information because you encourage them to do so?

5. Do you make it a habit to inquire beyond the reports, to enlarge your information base beyond the obvious?

6. Does your pursuit of information have a stimulating effect on those about you, as opposed to their feeling you are prying?

7. Can you generally enter into a decision-making situation with the assurance that the salient information is in your hands?

SOME HAVE IT, SOME DON'T

I have a healthy admiration for thorough and orderly business operations. My skills in these areas do not always match my admiration. But I do try; and I sometimes have to admit to failure.

The secret is in having as much work as possible reduced to a system. That's why the organizing and planning skills covered earlier are so important. Finding boxes and pigeonholes for activities on a regular basis eliminates a lot of day-to-day decision making. Putting standard due dates on reports helps get those reports in on time; it eliminates the annoying need for reminders. By standardizing work assignments and paper flow, the job is simplified. Once a system is adopted by everyone in an organization, friction is minimized.

Written policies and procedures along with accurately rendered organization charts and job descriptions are evidences of thoroughness and orderliness. Effort once expended on such matters saves repetition. The regular scheduling of expected staff meetings lets participants plan their time around them and minimizes the necessity of calling people in on the spur of the moment. In large organizations, a newsletter, or house organ can regularize distribution of important communications. Thoroughness and orderliness touch nearly every facet of managerial effort.

Watch the thorough and orderly manager at work. He has a minimum of paper on his desk because he knows that he can work on only one piece at a time. Ask him for something current, and he has it in a folder near at hand. Ask him for something that has been completed, and he'll identify its location in a flash. Give him a memo on a project, and he'll slip it into a current folder or put it in the appropriate file basket.

Watch such a manager open his briefcase. It isn't packed for a three-week trip. Instead, it resembles his desk, with the papers sorted into folders, ready for use. He may have some current literature in there and writing tools, but it's not a wastebasket. As an aside, I recall one pretender with whom I was associated. He always acted as though he lugged work home every night. One evening, he dropped his briefcase on his way out of the office. The contents were interesting: his rubbers, two half-eaten candy bars, a copy of *Esquire*, and a crossword-puzzle book. Pretenders are alive and well in every corporation!

Of course, orderliness can become a fetish. I have seen managers who were overly tidy and therefore never allowed work to progress at its full pace. I have seen managers who were so thorough that simple projects developed into major efforts—all out of proportion to their importance. These managers pull a minus impact value.

Plus impact managers are those who launch projects with a definite objective in mind. They get people working on tasks that can be fitted together into a complete job. They insist on interim progress reports and from time to time check to see what's happening. The people in such a work group expect to be checked on and, indeed, welcome it.

I recall one time apologizing to a worker for constantly checking on a project that was of particular concern to me. He laughed and said, "George, if you didn't check, I'd be disappointed." Then he added, "When you check up on what's happening, and I can show you that things are coming along well, you're checking on the job—not me."

Workers need that feeling. Since that one experience, I've tried to make it clear that it's job progress I'm interested in, not spying on the individual. McGregor's Theory X manager sees workers as people who need to have it all laid out for them and require prodding to get the task done. But his Theory Y manager sees workers as people who enjoy and take pride in achievement. The manager who can translate feelings about orderliness and thoroughness to workers, so that they take satisfaction in doing it that way, is the manager who generates impact two ways: in properly accomplished work and in constructively established relationships.

The same effective manager impresses his bosses with his own orderliness and thoroughness. They gain a feeling of confidence in him, knowing he'll deliver what he promises. It's that kind of trust that opens the way for bigger and better assignments.

Interim Impact Inventory

1. Do you have, and observe, written policies and procedures to cover the operation of your department?

2. Do you have organization charts or tables that clearly identify lines of reporting and levels of responsibility?

3. Is every job in your organization covered with a job description describing the function for which the job was created?

4. Do people in the organization adhere to the job descriptions and organization plans devised to control the work patterns?

5. Can you claim that day-to-day operations are systematic and can continue to function without specific instructions or in your absence?

6. Are your staff meetings held on a predictable and regular basis as opposed to being hastily called on a haphazard schedule?

7. Do you have a followup system that allows you to maintain ready checks on the progress of various projects assigned to subordinates?

8. Do your subordinates expect, understand, and even welcome your interim checks on their progress?

9. Do you work at an uncluttered desk, and can you find needed papers readily?

10. Is there a workable file system in your office, and can you find items in your secretary's absence?

11. Are your office and the departmental work areas generally clean and neat?

NO DECISION, NO ACTION—NO MANAGER

It is one thing to know how to make a decision and quite another to be willing to make one. Decision making is inherent in a number of areas, most significantly those discussed in the earlier sections of this book on knowledge and skill and the ability to apply them. The purpose here is not to elaborate on the decision-making process (it is assumed that is part of your basic skill package). It is the willingness to make decisions and the manner in which decisions are set forth that are important impact items. These aspects of decisiveness do deserve comment.

The speed with which decisions are made is often the mark of an effective manager. By that, I don't mean that one must always make fast decisions; there are times when delay is the best decision to make. For instance, I have had several experiences in which someone has come in with what appeared to be a problem calling for action: "Shouldn't we do something about that?" My response has sometimes been, "Sure, we'll talk about it first thing tomorrow."

And we do talk about it the following day. By then, there may have been a change in the nature of the problem, or it turns out that there was no problem in the first place. Meanwhile, everyone has had a chance to look at the matter from several angles. Fast action in such an instance could have sent us down the wrong path. But this is not always the case. Sometimes there isn't any running room, and fast action is in order.

The important thing for a manager to determine is whether delaying favors the gathering of facts until a more definitive decision is possible. That, in itself, is a decision. Anyone who knows and appreciates the decision-making process of identifying the problem, looking at the facts involved, coming up with a series of alternative actions, and deciding on one best action frequently hopes that more time were available. Certainly, the more thorough the process, the better the decision.

But there are situations where time is not available. Even then, unless it is a split-second matter (the ship is sinking fast!), the effective manager marshalls as much information and counsel as possible. He might even set in motion two actions to permit a better state of readiness only to cancel one later. He cannot delay; he must decide. He does.

Young managers would do well to study the backgrounds of old hands to see what it is that makes them ready for decision at a moment's notice. Is it intuition? Is it a disregard for the formalities of the process? In my mind, it is neither. In the absence of time to mull over facts and alternatives, the experienced manager reaches back into memory for similar situations. He knows that certain problems tend to lie behind certain conditions. If he can pin down the most likely of them, he's well on his way. That's because five years ago *that* problem was solved by applying *this* action.

There's also a danger in that, much as we admire the manager's evident capability. That danger is that an experienced manager might rely too much on what he did years ago, only to miss out on new ways of solving new problems and seizing new opportunities. The best managers I've ever worked with always took their time, if time was available. They always went through the whole process. And they always came up with good decisions!

The manager's day is filled with decisions—little ones as well as big ones. Priority setting is a decision. Which person to assign to what job is a decision. Most are made with thought, care, and time. Again, our emphasis is on a manager's planning and organizing skills. The better the overall planning, the fewer panic decisions will have to be made.

I have seen very bright people who could not make it to management level because, in the minds of their bosses, they could not make decisions. It's pathetic to see someone like that go into a top manager's office with three carefully planned programs for review. The manager says, "Which do you think will work best?" The poor subordinate won't commit himself and will begin to review all three with equal emphasis, ultimately throwing the matter on the boss's desk for disposition. I've heard managers say of people like that, "I'd promote Walter in a minute if, just for once, he could make up his mind."

Some managers won't make decisions until and unless they're forced into it. When I sold advertising, I would often have to leave copy and layout for internal review. Repeated calls would do little but draw the comment, "We're still studying it. It looks pretty good, but we'll tell you tomorrow." I would sometimes force the decision by saying, "Tomorrow is the last day I can get that to the magazine." When I picked it up again on the following day, it was often lying precisely where it had been put a week earlier. When it was too late to make changes, the original idea was accepted. Forced decisions are really not decisions. They're abdications.

Managers can develop decision-making prowess in subordinates by involving them in the process. Again, I'm touting participative management. Encourage others to bring their ideas into council. Let them see and hear the evaluative process. Let them see how the manager finally crystalizes a decision. It's important in the total development of an organization to let people see the innards of decision making.

There are managers who see themselves as self-sufficient and in no need of counsel. They misunderstand the function of the participative session. Although it is led democratically by the manager, the final decision is his. Decisions may be reached by a group because they are guided by the manager. Rather than rob from a manager's impact, this approach adds to it.

The last thing an effective manager can be is indecisive. The next last thing he can afford to be is a decider of wrong actions. The payoff comes in two directions: in the work that is accomplished and in the admiration people hold for the manager. Sometimes they go hand in hand.

Interim Impact Inventory

1. Are you willing to make a decision for which you take full responsibility, including credit for its success and criticism for its failure?

2. Do you assemble facts and evaluate them carefully before you form conclusions?

3. Can you generally attach priorities to issues demanding your decisions, moving quickly on some matters and more slowly on others?

4. Can you consult with others regarding decisions you must make without leaving the impression that you are ducking the ultimate responsibility?

5. Have you developed the skill of formulating a plan of action that has an alternative or fallback provision?

6. Do you sometimes make decisions in advance of need, anticipating the requirement of speedy action?

7. Do you make specific proposals for your boss's approval, as opposed to dumping all possible alternatives on him for him to make a decision?

8. Can you reverse an earlier decision on which new facts have come to light without embarrassment or defensiveness?

9. Do you involve subordinates in decision making, from both the fact-gathering and evaluative points of view, and do they see this as developmental?

BEYOND THE BLUE HORIZON

Chicken Little had no sense of perspective. Little Bo-Peep did. When Chicken Little felt the nut fall on her head, she stirred up the whole barnyard with her claim that the sky was falling. You know managers like that. Little Bo-Peep, on the other hand, didn't know where to find her sheep, so she reached back into her experience and concluded that the sheep would probably find *her*. You also know managers like that.

A sense of perspective is the ability to see things with a longer view, to see relationships in actions, and probably results and consequences. It keeps a manager from solving today's problem in ways that create new problems for tomorrow. It keeps him from ignoring little problems that may grow into major ones. In the ordering of priorities, it keeps him from putting the cart before the horse. It helps him emphasize important things, to change programs, policies, and procedures when they prove unworkable. It keeps him from making panic decisions and untenable commitments, and even saves him from legal battles.

In many cases, experience creates perspective. Yet I have seen experienced workers who have never developed it. They're the people of whom it's said, "He doesn't have 20 years of experience, just one year of experience 20 times." Some young people have it or develop it quickly. It's tied into the awareness we discussed earlier. Some people are just more circumspect than others.

The case-study method of instruction tends to develop perspective in learners more rapidly than the here's-how kind of teaching. Insights are developed at the same time other points of view are expressed. Again, it's a matter of seeing things in their proper relationships and taking the long-range view of present actions.

Managers who rise under the tutelage of managers with good perspective develop good perspective themselves. There is an argument here both for and against lines of succession. What begins well at the top can filter down to the bottom, and vice versa. I went through a few managers without perspective before I hit one with a truly good sense of it. The experience was at first mystifying, then exhilarating. Work is more satisfying under a manager who has a solid sense of perspective.

When Lincoln was confronted by the Temperance people about

General Grant's drinking, he wryly replied that if he knew what brand the winning general used, he'd send a case to each of the losers. How different this is from a sales manager I once knew who was concerned about punctuality and disliked salesmen who wandered off to make outside calls. Because of persistent hounding, his top salesman quit. He had been the wanderer. It might have been better for that manager to have rearranged schedules and encouraged everyone to make a few outside calls.

I recall a former client who spent inordinate amounts of money on incentives for salesmen when he should have been spending that money on improving the product. The firm ultimately went down the drain. I've seen labor contracts put together on an expedient basis without long-range consideration. I've seen departments created, only to discover later that they were superfluous, and other departments eliminated, only to discover later that they were indispensable.

Often, a lack of perspective generates personal problems for managers: They pursue career goals either beyond or short of their capabilities, or they make capricious moves, bad investments, and questionable alliances. It isn't unlike a game of chess, where the player plans moves not only with his own objectives in mind but also with thought given to the potential moves of the adversary. Perspective deals with today's actions in the light of future circumstances. We can't always predict, but we *can* preconsider.

Managers with a sense of perspective generate impact in at least two ways: their projects tend to come off with greater profit and with fewer surprises, and subordinates generate admiration for the manager whose leadership is steady and sure.

A sense of perspective takes time to develop and apply. It can be developed in the manager who builds the habit of thinking *several* steps ahead before taking step number one. Once developed, such planning becomes comfortable and second nature.

Interim Impact Inventory

1. Can you differentiate between small problems and big ones, and are you generally correct in your judgment?

2. Can you resist the panic and pressure for action sometimes urged on you by others?

3. Have you developed a chessplayer's ability to project one move into a sequence of moves and anticipate their consequences?

4. Can you resist that which is expedient in favor of the long-range view, however tempting an expedient may be?

5. Do you focus your attention on objectives and results rather than on the minutiae encountered along the way?

6. Can you generally go to the core of a problem without being detracted by peripheral matters?

7. Conversely, are you circumspect regarding the major effect minor influences can have on the outcome of an issue?

8. Do you attempt to develop a sense of perspective in your subordinates so that they see goals rather than merely perform tasks?

YOU CAN COUNT ON HIM

Not long ago I was discussing managerial predictability with a fairly successful young man who disagreed with my point of view. "I don't want my subordinates to anticipate my next move," he said. I *do*. I enjoy being able to anticipate my boss's reaction to problems I bring him, and I enjoy having people come to me with problems knowing pretty much how I'll react. In fact, once well established, the boss's point of view nearly becomes policy, and subordinates can often handle problems without constant consultation. That's how systems are born.

Predictability takes many forms. It may reflect a manager's temperament, habit patterns, business judgment, or moral and social views. In my opinion, the more predictable people are, the fewer conflicts arise and the smoother an operation becomes. After all, business operations are judged by what they yield in terms of productivity and profitability, not on the amount of turmoil they can generate.

If Jackson is difficult to deal with in the morning, leave controversial subjects for after lunch. If he doesn't go for funny stories and chitchat, don't take up his time with trivia. If his blood pressure rises with certain subjects, learn to approach them with a careful plan that is carefully expressed. When a manager is predictable in these areas, whether we like him for it or not, at least we know how to adjust and cope with it.

I worked under a man one time who, when listening to what I had to say, turned sideways in his chair and stared out the window. He concentrated that way; until I discovered that, I had the feeling he wasn't interested. Another manager I know closes his office door for the first half hour of each day, even though he has a completely open-door attitude at other times. It's his way of getting the day started properly. When you understand and accept them, patterns can at least be coped with.

Not long ago, I met a friend of mine for lunch. He was smarting over a confrontation he had had with his boss that morning. It seemed that a routine matter had been handled in much the same way as it had for years, but this particular action aborted. When my friend explained to his manager why he had done what he had done, the boss flew into a rage: "I expect to be consulted on problems of that sort before any action is ever taken." This was a complete reversal of the position he had held for so long—"Just handle those things as they come up. Don't bother me."

Because I come in contact with many managers in many different phases of the business, I try to pin down some of the attitudes that prevail for each. There are those who like to be consulted at length before any project is launched. And there are those who prefer to see a project plan reasonably well developed so that they can exercise approval or veto with as little investment of their time as possible. For one manager, I do one thing; for the other, it's quite a different approach. Knowing in advance what the manager likes or dislikes not only results in more productivity but makes for a simpler and more pleasant relationship.

Interpersonal relationships in business are best when they have a constancy. The strategy, then, becomes more straightforward and the tactics less devious. Managers who choose to be elusive, inconsistent, and unpredictable are generally those who believe that, when a worker is "on tilt," he's also "on his toes." My own observations are that workers whose concerns are largely focused on second-guessing the boss do not spend enough time in solving the real problems of the business.

Predictability works in all directions and accelerates productivity. It minimizes surprises. It saves time. It cuts down on frustration and simplifies relationships. Since it can do all that, it's certainly worth a few more impact points!

Interim Impact Inventory

1. Are you generally of an even disposition, not given to extreme highs or lows in thought or action?

2. Do you see evidence of subordinates taking action predicated on their prejudgments of your approval?

3. Do you take the same posture with all your subordinates and maintain that posture for extended periods of time?

4. Do subordinates, peers, and superiors work with you in an open, direct manner, as opposed to an obvious testing-the-environment approach?

5. When you do take on a different point of view or a different mode of operation, do you make it clear to others that there has been a change?

6. Is the atmosphere of your work area a reflection of your constancy of behavior?

SHORT FUSES BURN HOT, NOT BRIGHT

The manager who can't control himself can't control others. Predictable as he may be, we don't enjoy being in his company. There's a lot of time wasted when people have to wait for the dust to settle after an emotional outburst.

Perhaps it's the teacher in me that places great value on patience and composure. Indeed, you must be patient if you expect to teach, because people can't always see the light in a uniform way or at the same time. Nor will they agree with a particular point of view. Managers, if they are constructive, spend a lot of time explaining, teaching, coaching, and counseling—all of which require patience. And they are often put into the position of listening to varied points of view—all of which require an element of composure. True impact managers have at least reasonable levels of both.

The highly directive manager slides past this requirement at the very outset. He doesn't bother with instructing; he simply gives orders. He doesn't listen to other points of view; he just expresses his own. Perhaps he earns enough points on vigor and endurance to obviate the need for other points. In the end, he loses the game because of the repeated failures of his subordinates and misses out on the valuable points of view that others can bring to the job.

It isn't easy to go over a project laboriously with someone only to sense that that person, who will have to do the job, doesn't understand it. Maybe he does understand it, but he doesn't see the necessity for doing it. Or he doesn't want to do it on your time schedule or in your way. I know there are some managers who would say: "Tough. Let him work it out. It has to be done when I want it and how I want it. And it'll get done because I want it." I understand the exasperation but disagree with the position.

If people don't understand a task, they usually do it poorly. If they aren't sold on its necessity, they do it reluctantly. If they're forced into doing it a way that doesn't make sense to them, they find a way to prove that it shouldn't be done that way. Remember the grocery-store boys and the area supervisor? People find a way to fight back.

The smart money is on the manager who can keep his cool and go through the necessary explanatory and motivational steps to assure a performance that is both enlightened and willing. That takes patience. And if the manager encourages a free exchange of ideas, he's likely to encounter well-expressed opposition. That takes composure.

Managers have to enter into problem-solving and work-assigning situations with the understanding that they have a significant advantage over those they will be leading in the activity. First, they have undoubtedly thought about the need for action for some time. Second, their position gives them primary responsibility and authority. Third, they are assumed to know more about what has to be done than their subordinates—and why. Patience and composure bridge those gaps.

Patience is important in other ways, as well. It's the backup for conviction in many situations. For instance, a project the manager felt was so important, so well planned and executed, fizzles. Going back and repairing, rescheduling, and reexecuting are annoying and embarrassing. The conviction that it was the right thing to do in the first place still clings. Patience allows a second try.

The exponents of Transactional Analysis put patience high on the list of adult characteristics and lack of it on the list of child qualities. What better way is there to describe a manager than to say that he took an adult view or acted in an adult way?

Admittedly, patience and composure have their limits. There comes a time when there may be validity in announcing that you've come to the end of explanations and excuses. In fact, the ultimate reversal of form may point up the fact that much patience and composure has been invested in the project and that the manager isn't going to be endlessly charitable. That's the end game, however, not the opening gambit.

The best work I've ever done has been accomplished under patient managers. Their willingness to take time in getting jobs started properly paid off in their getting the jobs completed properly. Their willingness to give the needed time to a project to assure quality paid off in quality results. Their ability to accept defeat with a resolve to try again made the second time more effective. I never saw such managers fail. I always enjoyed being in their company. I could take direction or criticism from them because I knew it was carefully, patiently considered.

My first inclination is not to be patient. But experience has taught me that there isn't any substitute for keeping my cool. Again, patience is a learned skill. There's a risk while learning, because while the manager practices, others often wonder whether he doesn't know or doesn't care. It's time-consuming, and that taxes patience all the more. But it impacts properly on productivity and on relationships as well. That makes developing the skill well worth it.

Interim Impact Inventory

1. When you encounter a mistake in judgment or action, is your first thought directed at getting the matter corrected, as opposed to telling off the person who made the error?

2. Can you teach and reteach without exasperation?

3. Are you willing to spend time in explaining so as to preclude misunderstandings or opposition?

4. Are you able to listen to an opposing point of view—one you believe demonstrates the other person's lack of understanding—without interrupting and taking over?

5. Can you stick with a problem and pull out a workable solution without blowing up in the process?

6. Do you have a stabilizing effect on others, keeping your head even though they lose theirs?

7. Do people come to you to discuss problems, knowing you'll counsel with them rather than take over?

8. When all resources have been exhausted and you do fly off the handle, do people agree that you had a right to do so?

NOW THAT'S A GREAT IDEA

Creativity in management is broader than its dictionary definition implies. Indeed, the most creative people I know are those for whom life in management would be difficult, if not impossible. Modern management imposes the restrictions of policies, procedures, routines, and obligations, all of which can fence in the writer, the painter, or the musician—people in acknowledged creative professions.

Yet there are many creative people within the ranks of management. They are the innovators of products, the changers of methods of marketing, the developers of sophisticated manufacturing devices, or the architects of huge, multinational enterprises. Much as we joke about creative accounting, there are those who have made innovations in the field of recordkeeping and reporting—all to the benefit of those who have to interpret and make judgments regarding financial matters.

Creative managers can be the ones who initiate processes, but they can also be the individuals who recognize a good idea when they see it. They are also the people who can tie two ideas into a workable combination. They encourage creative input in volume, because they have the capacity to sift through a variety of suggestions and come up with one complete and workable way to go. They are the managers who listen and look at things, reserving critique until last.

The brainstorming techniques that became popular in the 1950s opened the eyes of many managers. Of course, many also looked on the concept as nonsense. But this approach, to gather people around a table and generate multiple ideas regarding a single problem (where "hitchhiking" is accepted and positive or negative comments are prohibited), continues to be practiced in subtle ways by managers who believe in participative management. Group creativity, encouraged by a manager, earns that manager the label "creative."

Over the years, my own work has put me face to face with both creative and uncreative managers. I hasten to add that my judgment as to which was which hasn't always been predicated on whether or not they agreed with me. One creative manager was a college president for whom I put together promotional pieces and fund-raising material. Because it was a conservative institution, my inclination was to be conservative. His idea was to break gently but visibly from that mold. We did so bit by bit. And it was invigorating to work in such a climate.

On the uncreative side, there was the executive for whom a bright, marketing-oriented group came up with a battery of product names, several of them ideally suited to the times. These were rejected in favor of a dull, prosaic name that was as ill-fitting as army boots on a ballerina. It had been his suggestion, of course. Then there was the manager who clung to antiquated training-program content and techniques simply because that was the way it had been when he joined the company. Or the manager who let a whole market slip away simply because he couldn't see how people in a given earnings bracket could afford, let alone be interested in, his services.

Admittedly, a lot of brilliant, highly creative ideas have backfired. The only real proof of it is when a good idea is rejected by one person and later accepted by another who makes it work. The creative manager will at least take a look and, maybe, give a new idea a try.

If the manager is either an idea generator or an idea appreciater, it's a big plus in his favor. He'll make his department or his company an exciting place to work. He'll build admiration among his associates—above, below, and alongside. Best of all, he'll probably be a step ahead of his competition rather than somewhere behind it.

Impact is earned by the manager who creates some of his own.

Interim Impact Inventory

1. Do you enjoy taking new looks at old practices, however well accepted they may be?

2. Do you encourage people in your work group to discuss innovations with you?

3. Do you accept and give recognition to new ideas, even if they aren't your own?

4. Have you the talent for taking two or three good ideas and welding them into a blockbuster of a plan?

5. Are you willing to throw out last year's smash hit, perhaps your idea at the time, in favor of a new suggestion by someone else?

6. Will you help a creative subordinate refine an idea, even if at the outset you are in doubt about its chances of success?

7. Can you discipline your creativity and resist making constant changes when an earlier good idea is making good progress?

INTEGRITY IS ITS OWN REWARD

Day in and day out, metropolitan newspapers carry stories of unacceptable moral behavior on both the corporate and personal levels. We read of cheating, payoffs, bribes, stealing, unsavory connections, and a variety of questionable affairs. Some of them involve individuals; others are traceable to corporate entities.

A careful reading of history tells us this is not a recent phenomenon. We suffered from it in other days and in other ways, too. What may be a healthy aspect of it, however, is that it is being exposed and disciplined more widely and publicly now. Major corporations, particularly those that are aware of adverse public reaction and subsequent economic penalties, write careful policies aimed at controlling behavior within acceptable standards.

Even the most carefully written policies and laws meet problems in interpretation. One person's ethics may be considerably more or less stringent than another's. For some, morality is a set of absolutes and imperatives. For others, it is a loosely tied set of maybes. Ethics and morality are part of a code of principles that defines right and wrong, good or evil. Although I would argue in favor of my own point of view, I'm well aware that others can just as convincingly argue their own. What is bedrock truth to me may be seen by another as quicksand. Again, we are faced with subjectivity.

Integrity can be viewed more objectively. Integrity is how you adhere to a set of principles. It takes ethics into the arena where the game is really played. It can even be translated into actions with no carefully defined moral code to support them. In other words, a manager who does not necessarily think a lot or talk a lot about honesty can be extremely honest. That's just his way of doing things.

Room should be left here to accommodate the inadvertent or ill-advised action. Perfection always seems to elude us. The Apostle Paul lamented that he did things he shouldn't do—and didn't do things he should. He wasn't happy about it and worked against his failings. An objective look at integrity should therefore embrace conscious and observable behavioral changes toward higher standards.

In a business setting, integrity works on different levels. For the employee: Do the boss's directions require sacrifice or compromise of my personal set of ethics? For the manager: Do the actions of my associates or subordinates reflect a level of ethics incompatible with my own? The happiest arrangement, obviously, is that in which people are not made uncomfortable and don't have to struggle with conscience.

In my own business experience, I've been spared the problem of being directed to do anything that went against my own principles. This is a tribute to the many fine managers with whom I've been associated. They had either the integrity to avoid unacceptable activity or the good judgment to keep from testing mine. In any case, I have been fortunate in working under, with, and around men and women of character and trust. When you don't have to be troubled by a lack of integrity surrounding you, more time and effort can be spent on getting the job done.

Lots of little things are swept into the integrity classification. For instance, can an employee confide in the manager with assurance that private thoughts won't become public gossip? Can the manager put confidential material into another's hands with the assurance that it won't be used indiscriminately? Can this or that person be trusted with company money, the company's reputation, or company confidences? Is behavior predictable and compatible with the manager's principles and the company's policies?

The manager's role is to facilitate work. To the extent that he is able to make subordinates respect, trust, and feel comfortable with him, he accelerates the work process. We don't find that kind of motivated effort in organizations where the manager is the center of criticism or uneasiness.

I've seen organizations headed by managers of questionable integrity. One manager was always gloating about some slick deal he'd put over on someone. (Would you like to deal with him?) Another was quick to compromise the confidences of others. (Would you discuss a personal problem with him?) A third was an artist at reporting only data that made him look good. (Would you rely on his information?) A fourth sought to generate loyalty by pitting people against each other. (Who does he pit against you?) Still another was openly critical of subordinates who committed minor indiscretions while he, 150 miles away from home, committed major ones. (Would you take criticism from him?)

The storybook ending of the above examples would have each of them falling, drummed out of the corps. Some did, others didn't. Each failed, though, in the sense that productivity in the department was lessened by the lack of respect and trust the workers showed them. Impact, in my opinion, builds in direct proportion as respect and trust grow. Integrity—the application of ethics and the demonstration of morality—can earn that kind of impact!

Interim Impact Inventory

1. Are your own standards of behavior within the parameters of the standards you know to be acceptable in your own company?

2. Do you make an honest attempt to behave in accordance with such standards?

3. Would it be difficult for someone to get something on you regarding your general behavior?

4. So far as you know, do you protect your subordinates from situations that might cause a breach of their behavior standards?

5. Can subordinates, peers, and superiors confide in you with the same sense of security they might have with their doctors or lawyers?

6. Do you make it clear to your subordinates that you expect them to maintain high levels of integrity as they deal with you?

7. Would you say that your integrity is generally well respected?

A POINT WORTH REMEMBERING

I suppose memories do fade with age. Yet I had an uncle who, at 85, could recite more poetry, quote more philosophy, accurately recall more history, and come up with more current data than anyone I've ever known sixty years his junior. What happens with adults is that they either don't feel the necessity of maintaining a sharp memory or they become very selective in the things they memorize.

While becoming a human data bank isn't necessary for the effective manager, there are certain basic areas in which memory should be developed. The first of these is a facility with names. Another is the ability to recall the central themes of significant events. Certainly, an effective manager will want to be able to produce, quickly, the current and relevant data associated with a present activity. Among the more interesting managers I have known are those who have the ability to trot out, as needed, illustrations, stories, and even colorful trivia to make their points.

Remembering names has obvious interpersonal value. Who doesn't like to have a respected manager call him by name? That speaks to one of life's most fundamental psychological needs, the sense of feeling important, accepted, and respected. For the manager who would generate impact on his own behalf, this is a priority skill. And it works up, down, and laterally.

Jim Farley, one-time postmaster general in the Roosevelt administration, was said to have the most fantastic memory for names in his time. He found it politically advantageous to do so. A former associate minister in our church with a congregation of 4,500 people could stand in the foyer after services and name nearly every one of his parishioners. The average manager may not have to be able to put on so flashy a demonstration, but he should be able to handle the names of his immediate workers and associates, also those of his regular customers, vendors, and acquaintances.

Often an event comes up in conversation, and how nice it is to have people remember it, particularly if it was a significant one. Most important is being able to recall what that event meant in terms of the business or private lives of the individuals concerned.

When *you* remember what *I* remember, a vitally effective interpersonal compact is developed.

As with most managers, piles of information flow across my desk each day. Curiosity drives me to look at each piece at least cursorily. I read junk mail that way, as well as free literature in banks, hotels, and lobbies of offices. I'm a sucker for annual reports and house organs. Occasionally, something hits me that's worth remembering; more often, this kind of information runs out at the same rate it comes in.

We also learn to be selective in what we keep in our mental data banks as regards business reports and memoranda. Some we note and file. Some we scan and discard. Some we read carefully and remember. It's folly to try to take in and save everything. Yet the most impressive managers I know are those who don't have to run to the files in every conversation with them. They save file reference for those occasions when specific information is absolutely required. What is more interesting is when file matches memory and memory holds up well.

Earlier, we discussed a manager's formal and conversational speaking skills. Here, again, memory plays an important part. When a speaker wants to make a point or respond to a question, a treasury of available stories or illustrations is valuable. I'm always in search of new ones, because I need them in my work. But so do other managers. I know many effective managers who can lean back in their chairs and tell a little anecdote that fits the situation, makes the point they want to make, and then wins the argument for them.

Managers who remember are remembered. Both data and personal information are important. Being able to recall things without searching the files is impressive as well as time saving. Being able to remember the names of workers, their spouses and children, their interests and problems makes for a more human relationship between boss and worker. Making notes on a calendar pad is good business, but it doesn't come off particularly well in interpersonal situations.

A good memory is a necessary skill for an impact manager. It's developable. It's important. It makes for impact both on the job and away from it. It's something managers have to have if they are to function effectively.

Interim Impact Inventory

1. Is your memory for names such that you are seldom, if ever, embarrassed?

2. Do you remember the names of the wives and children of your close associates?

3. Can you make an informal presentation involving data without the need for voluminous notes?

4. Can you be selective in what you feel should be remembered and what should be filed away from reference?

5. Do you have a ready store of illustrations and anecdotes to add interest and meaning to your communications?

6. Do you remember (or have a memory-jogging system) for important dates, such as birthdays and anniversaries?

7. If memory has ever been a problem for you, have you ever taken a course, read a book, or otherwise attempted to improve this skill?

BEING SOMBER IS NO LAUGHING MATTER

Gloomy people are no fun to be around. People who can't make a joke or take a joke make miserable company. There is no business, no business circumstance that can't profit from a measure of optimism and a sense of humor. They are important, not only for interpersonal relationships but for the good mental health of all concerned.

People should take their work seriously, but not themselves. We may not laugh at mistakes in business, but we also can't afford to let them prevent easy transitions while they're being corrected. The manager can, and should, set the pace in this. If success is what we're looking for when we launch a project, then an air of optimism should prevail. Here, too, it's the manager's optimism that should be up front.

The sales manager who broods about sales slumps will find his pessimism is contagious. Shaking the head and moaning about market factors or competition doesn't motivate a sales force. Neither does it impress a boss who is looking for improvement. But optimism, coupled with some realistic effort, makes a fine combination. It motivates and leads—the manager's role. People like to work for a manager who can shrug off disappointment, roll up his sleeves, and go at it again.

There seems to be a correlation between the manager who is optimistic and the manager with a sense of humor. Test this, if you will, with the pessimist. Pick a tense moment and introduce a little levity. You'll find yourself with a totally unreceptive audience. Try it with the optimist, and you'll not only have him respond, but he's likely to chip in with some humor himself.

A quick illustration of two very real managers: One was the complete pessimist, devoid of humor. The other was optimistic and always ready to let a light moment punctuate his day.

First, the humorless manager. Not only could he not laugh at himself, he couldn't laugh at anything. His key people complained of a string of maladies, including high blood pressure, ulcers, failing eyesight, and shortness of breath. To my unpracticed eyes, there were a few nervous breakdowns in the making. His subordinates made every excuse possible to keep away from his office. Many of them took the very first transfer available to them, even if it wasn't their first career choice. He impacted negatively on them and, unfortunately, in later years, on himself.

The other manager, in the same company and at the same time, had a quiet, warm sense of humor. He worked hard, and his subordinates worked hard. Whereas the people in the first manager's department functioned out of fear, this manager's people worked cooperatively and constructively. This was a no-nonsense business, but there was always a minute or two for an amusing anecdote. If the boss misspoke, he laughed at himself. If someone got uptight over a problem in the shop, this manager heard him out, helped him out, and found a light way to cap off the incident. Under which kind of manager would the greatest productivity be expected?

A good manager doesn't have to be a raconteur, a master of the one liner or the life of the party. He doesn't have to be funny, just receptive to some of the funnier things that pass his way. He can be dead serious about his business, but he's dead wrong if he doesn't think funny things happen in his store, factory, or office.

When a worker enjoys being in his manager's presence, doesn't feel uncomfortable when discussing problems or admitting mistakes, a more honest, open transaction of business is likely to take place. Today's managers need all the openness and honesty they can get from the organization, so encouraging them with some optimism and humor is just good sense. The manager with a smile is approachable, and that's where is all begins.

Your sense of humor has to be controlled if it's to be effective. It has to be understood by others as a sense of humor and not as frivolity. Lincoln, whose sense of humor kept him upright during the dark days of the Civil War, was often seen as a buffoon by those who had no sense of humor. It's an impact factor that must be applied with a great deal of circumspection.

A sense of humor also has to be properly pointed; inward is better than outward. The manager who laughs at himself or includes himself in the joke is better off than the one who makes fun of others. Thomas Carlyle had an interesting thought on this when he said that humor wasn't from the head but from the heart. It's not contempt, but love. It is shown less in laughs than in smiles. Enjoying humor is what I am talking about, not creating it at someone else's expense.

Truly big people are big enough not to be damaged by laughing at themselves once in a while. Nor are they damaged when they laugh at oddball events that happen in their places of business. What they can't afford is to be so humorless that others laugh at them in unkind ways.

A ready smile and a hearty laugh—at the right time and with the right audience—are worthwhile impact material.

Interim Impact Inventory

1. Are people in your organization generally open and at ease in your presence?

2. Do you maintain an optimistic view of your business by looking at success in the long run despite periodic difficulties?

3. Do the people in your organization reflect your optimism by working hard to prove it?

4. Can you laugh off a mistake—yours or one of your subordinates'—yet seriously determine not to repeat it?

5. Do you relate incidents to others in which you were the object of humor or embarrassment?

6. Can you keep your anecdotes on others from being sarcastic or damaging to them?

7. Can you tell the difference between people laughing with you as opposed to at you?

Part 4
Impact Add-ons
That Rise out of Attitudes

TURNING ANOTHER CORNER

The previous sections focused on a manager's personal qualities and his ability to employ them. Most of them portrayed a decent person, a circumspect individual with whom one could work with a sense of comfort and assurance. It should be pointed out again that we look for effectiveness in a manager; being considered a "nice" person is merely an added benefit. However, the qualities listed have a very important place in the impact pattern.

The personal qualities that occupied our attention to this point are those that establish and support relationships in a way that enables a manager's leadership abilities to prevail. Put another way, they allow a manager to lead. The more of these qualities managers can put together, the more predictable will their effectiveness be in gathering the support of the people they work with.

Now we'll briefly explore a number of managerial attitudes that add further dimension to a manager's impact. They show how the manager perceives himself, his job, and other people with whom he has contact. As these attitudes are applied, the manager is seen in turn by others who make judgments and react to him. Favorable judgments and positive reactions create an environment in which it becomes possible to manage effectively.

These attitudes take on a slightly different flavor from the qualities discussed earlier. Although many continue to enhance relationships, others tend to set the spirit and the pace of work to be done. Whereas discussion of other qualities may have left the impression that it is desirable to have "nice-minded" management, the attitudes dealt with here will focus largely on firm-minded management.

It takes a well-rehearsed actor to conceal attitudes. Most people we meet in business don't have such skills, nor do they attempt to demonstrate them. Similarly, most managers we know don't do very much pretending. They feel entitled to certain attitudes and the right to reveal them. Yet I have watched management attitudes change, some of them for the good and some for the worse. Just as we can mold qualities, so we can mold attitudes.

Looking ahead, we can see that some attitudes (as we saw in some personal qualities) are potential danger areas. Properly applied and adequately controlled, they can be tremendously beneficial. Improperly applied and controlled, they can be damaging. Now let's take a look at some of these attitude factors and see how they can affect a manager's impact.

SELF-CONFIDENCE, THE PERSONAL POWER SOURCE

Self-confidence is an asset and a virtue in the manager's toolbox, but it must measure up to certain standards if it is to be worth much. First, it has to be based on fact. The manager must honestly feel—and be able to support the feeling with performance—that he is up to the task. To the extent that the manager fools himself on his adequacy, he magnifies his inadequacy in the minds of his associates and subordinates.

A second measure of self-confidence is in the manner in which it's expressed. Quiet, firm expressions and demonstrations do it best. Boasting and displays of vanity *un*do it. Here we could get into a mixture of semantics and theology, because pride is considered by many to be the most insidious kind of sin. On a more practical level, though, self-confidence that comes off as "Hey, look at me" turns others off, not on!

Another view of self-confidence is that it shouldn't be masked in a veil of humility. This is another quasitheological area in which I have strong feelings but will not comment on at length. In the Puritan ethic, humility is the personal putdown that pretends to heighten virtue in direct proportion to the amount of misery one can accumulate. That's bad enough. But when self-confidence is masked with "Aw shucks, it's nothing" or "I'm not sure I can do it" (knowing full well that you can), it's phony. I like C. S. Lewis's statement that humility is not thinking badly of yourself, it's just not thinking of yourself at all.

Not long ago, a young man I know and appreciate for his sound qualities was given a significant promotion. I asked if he thought he was up to it. His answer was, "I've got my work cut out for me, but there's nothing in that job I haven't had a chance to look at and be familiar with. I'll want to change some things, and that will take time. It'll be different working this from the top rather than from the middle. But once the transition is made and the priorities are set, I'm sure it'll go well. Yes, I look forward to it."

That's quiet, reasoned self-confidence. Nothing dashing and flashy about it, just studied certainty. There's nothing in that attitude that might retard his forward movement. Also, there's nothing in it that might prompt a turn-off by those with whom he is associated. In fact, I predict excellent cooperation and progress for that young man in his first substantial foray into the management field.

I've known other young managers who have taken stronger or weaker approaches to this kind of situation. Some have been so supremely (and mistakenly) self-confident that they plunged in, stirred up wasp's nests all over the place, became overextended, and failed. Others moved in with such fear and trepidation that they lost hold of the situation immediately. The middle road of acting sure because you feel sure, then playing it that way without a lot of noise is the truer, more self-confident way to go.

Self-confidence is the steam in the boiler. Without it, no wheels can turn, and no progress can be made. Let it get out of control, and the boiler bursts. It's that simple.

Self-confidence feeds on itself. As self-confident managers see they are right, they move forward with even more courage. So do those who work with them. It's a contagious and constructive attitude that ultimately permeates an organization. And that's impact!

Interim Impact Inventory

1. Do you move into the more difficult aspects of your job with the feeling that you can see them through?

2. Do your subordinates recognize your abilities without your reminding them of how capable you are?

3. Can you accept a compliment without the pretense of humility and without crowing either?

4. As your experience grows, do you reflect an even stronger, more justifiable sense of self-confidence?

5. Can you display your self-confidence to others without the hint of arrogance or superiority?

6. When your self-confidence is threatened, do you make an honest attempt to restore it by working off the deficiency that threatened it?

I WANT TO BE AND I'M WILLING TO DO

Ambition, like self-confidence, is the kind of attitude that can be either constructive or destructive. In its worst sense, ambition is selfishness. In its best sense, it is expansive. I've seen a few managers with the kind of ambition that plagued Julius Caesar, and I've watched a few of them fall as hard as Caesar did. That's not the sort of ambition I'd prescribe for the effective impact manager we're looking for.

This is not to say that an overly ambitious manager won't succeed. Indeed, there are wildly self-centered, ambitious managers who let nothing stand in their way; and they often get to the top of the heap. But we should admit that these are people who probably had other things going for them as well. In most cases, they probably moved so fast that others just stood by in amazement. Sure it works, but it's a risky business and not for everyone.

I recommend and applaud ambition in a manager. I like the person who says he is going to succeed and is willing to work at it. The second part of that statement is the qualifying one. When we discuss ambition, we have to add to it the factors of determination and perseverance.

Not long ago, a trainee in one of my seminars introduced himself as being in training for a vice presidency. Later I heard some grumbling, from both other trainees and some of the older hands. The young man's attitude was quite appropriate and he undoubtedly has just as much chance as anyone else in that group of becoming a V.P. His judgment was a little awry, however, because he failed to calculate the effect of his public declaration on those around him. Perhaps, too, there are people in the group who will work quite pointedly against his reaching his goal. We'll see.

Some managers let ambition be their Achilles heel. Either they incur the wrath of the peers and subordinates who undermine the manager's program of progress, or they undermine their own progress by looking so hard at the next job that they don't handle the present one effectively. In the latter case, it may not be entirely their fault, because sometimes high-profile people are placed in jobs with the understanding that such positions are merely developmental assignments. Their own managements have sown the idea of their just passing through, so they act accordingly. A lot of care has to be exercised by both parties in such arrangements.

Truly ambitious managers do a number of things to assure their own success. The first is to set long-range goals they feel are achievable. Never mind the hurdles ahead; they concentrate only on the personal issue of how well they can fill present job requirements. With that issue attended to, it's time to move to the next step in the plan to fulfill ambition.

Set interim goals and a reasonably acceptable time schedule. Can I be ready to take that next higher spot three years from now? Is it reasonable to believe that anyone else will think I'm ready for such a position? If I don't make it in three years, how much longer should I allow myself? Is it possible that I could be ready in two years if the opportunity presented itself? What do I have to do to get ready?

Set alternate paths. The one you may want to follow most may be blocked and foil your expectations. Jobs once considered stepping stones may change in concept and importance; they may no longer be viable routes to pursue. Business emphases can change, and your own ideas about yourself and your career may change with them. Alternatives make good sense in career planning, particularly when you consider that many influences are beyond your control.

Here is the clincher. How much effort, extra schooling, extra hours, and extra care are you willing to go along with to fulfill the contract you make with yourself? This is the point at which ambition often turns sour. Without the determination and perseverance required to pull it off, ambition becomes an impact robber. Most people view ambitious managers who want to go places but won't pay the fare as deadbeats, unworthy of support or cooperation.

It's the manager with ambition, but without the willingness to earn his way, who most frequently resorts to subverting others. He's the person who casts his opponents in a poor light, holds others back, takes credit for things others have accomplished, creates crises to come up with miraculous cures himself, and falsifies records to give himself a halo. It's done all the time and is easy to see. It works. Remember the old saw about keeping the ladder clean and tidy as you go up, because it may be slippery on the way down? I've watched it happen, and it's only poetic justice.

Properly ambitious managers make their own ambition contagious among their subordinates when they share the progress they make. "Let's make this department successful. Let's get people in this department properly credited for things they do. Let's pull this company up, and ourselves with it. Let's get some people promoted here to make room for other promotions within. I intend to go places, and you're coming along!"

Earlier we said that managers create a climate in which others *allow* them to manage. That's true of ambition too. Managers can pursue their ambitions with determination and perseverance as long as those who are responsible for their success allow it. Ambition isn't having a chip on the shoulder. It's a gut conviction that requires muscle to work it out.

Interim Impact Inventory

1. Have you ever set goals for yourself, and do you revise them realistically as circumstances change?

2. As you establish goals, do you also take cognizance of what it will require of you to achieve those goals?

3. Have you done the things you need to do in order to make those goals reachable, such as take courses and volunteer for tough assignments?

4. Do you see that the achievement of your objectives ties in with the achievements of those under your supervision?

5. Can you honestly say that your ambition will result in progress for your company as well as for yourself?

6. Do you pursue your ambitions in such a way that when you do achieve them you will be applauded and not criticized by subordinates, peers, and superiors?

MANAGING FOR QUALITY, VOLUME, AND PROFITABILITY

If we were to lay what's been said here on the Blake-Mouton Managerial Grid, it might easily be concluded that our emphasis has been heavily on the side of "concern for people." I suppose that's so, but it must be remembered that it's through people that we get work done. It's the sanction of employees that allows an employer to function. If we don't believe that, we go against some pretty formidable odds. Now let's look at the other side of the grid—concern for production.

Society in the form of the marketplace ultimately calls the tune to which we dance. It rightly demands a useful, worthwhile, workable, reasonably durable, and attractive product or service. Unless we produce such a product or service, people won't buy. But consumers put another pressure on our sweaty brows. They want exceptional products at the lowest possible prices.

Although businesspeople do want to provide their customers with exceptional products or services at low prices, they also want something else they deserve: profits. Managers find themselves in the middle, trying to satisfy both demands. Day in and day out, they juggle three balls—quality, volume, and profitability.

Effective managers make no bones about letting people know their attitudes; they want it all. They tell subordinates that, without adequate quality, people won't buy, and without adequate quantity, people won't wait. They don't see it as a trade-off between quality and quantity. They don't say, "Make them perfect, no matter how long it takes." They don't say, "Good or bad, I need 10,000 of these by tomorrow." They do say, "We need 10,000 high-quality pieces by tomorrow."

Before such an attitude can be expressed, a lot of other things have to be in place. Objectives have to be reasonable. The potential for achieving those objectives has to be enhanced by about a dozen characteristics, such as the know-how, personal qualities and personal attitudes I've already described. Here's where it all comes together. And if it doesn't come together here, there's been a great waste of time and energy.

Quality and quantity production begin with the manager. Sure, when at the end of the day there aren't enough pieces ready to ship, or quality is poor, some managers like to blame their subordinates. To that kind of manager, I pose these questions: Who hired these workers? Who trained them? Who supervised them? Show me bad quality coming off an assembly line, and I'll show you a manager who hasn't done his job well!

McGregor's Theory Y manager begins with the proper frame of mind. He says, "The workers in this department have the same pride in accomplishment I do. I'll see to it that I make it possible to achieve by encouraging them, helping them, and acknowledging their achievements when they occur." MBO managers bring the organization together. Along with volume objectives, they work out clear understandings of acceptable quality standards.

Herzberg shows us that a worker's greatest satisfaction is in doing the job itself. People tend to work harder and more carefully for a compliment than they do for money. One of the reasons why many managers never seem to agree with this is that they don't set adequate quality or volume standards in the first place, and they don't acknowledge achievement when it occurs. So they miss at both ends, and lose a tremendous opportunity to achieve themselves.

In my first teaching job many years ago, I asked students to turn in written assignments at certain intervals but gave no specific instructions on format or neatness. In other words, I set no quality standards. Somehow, I had convinced myself that they wouldn't respond to such instructions as "Turn in your assignments typewritten or carefully handwritten in ink on one side of the paper only." I paid for that mistake by spending a good part of that year deciphering pencil scrawls on an assortment of paper sizes and shapes.

The following year, I had a college senior assigned to me who would be doing his intern teaching under my supervision. On his first day in front of the class, he stated that the assignment was to be done on one side of the paper only, typed or written in ink. I could hardly conceal my amusement, and I decided he would discover for himself what a foolish request he had made. But the papers came in the next day precisely as he had requested them to be. From that day, I required the same standards and met with equal success. I learned from the young man I was supposed to teach that you don't get quality unless you ask for it.

In my General Electric experience, I recall a period in which an inordinate amount of scrap was being produced. It was simply a case of careless workmanship, producing less-than-quality products that were ultimately sent back by an inspection station. Back went the inferior items to be reworked, reinspected, or scrapped. Top management said that something had to be done.

What was done was not only very simple; it was appropriate to the situation. First, all employees were reminded what quality was required and why it had to be. Then, we posted a chart at the end of each line. On the chart was a simple statement: "We made this much scrap today." During the first week, scrap held to its old level. Then, as workers became interested, the figures on the graph showed a downward trend. Without a lot of management hoopla, the workers took it upon themselves to compete, one line against another. The scrap losses evaporated because most people don't like to be known as careless workers.

My uncle, an old-time steelmaker, tells the story of the steel-mill superintendent who came down at the end of the day shift and asked the straw boss how many heats had been done that day. The boss said, "Five." So the superintendent wrote the number 5 on the floor, with a big piece of chalk. When the night shift came on, someone asked what the 5 meant. "I hear that's how many heats the day shift did today," said one of the workers. The next morning, the 5 had been rubbed out and a big 6 was in its place. Competition again. As the days wore on, the numbers increased until they reached as high as 9. As the story goes, they never dropped back down to 5.

Effective management doesn't make people work harder than they should, but it does make people work as hard as they should. And it's not done from the viewpoint of the Theory X manager who says that people don't want to work and they have to be prodded. It's done from the Theory Y viewpoint that, when people are properly pointed, they like to achieve and put forth the skill, care, and effort needed to do it.

Poor management loses the game to workers. Prior to going to college, I worked for a year in the Carborundum Company plant at Niagara Falls. They made a fine product, but in those days we were still subject to an old-fashioned, highly directive, do-it-or-else kind of management. We did piecework and put in a considerable amount of overtime, because the nation was tooling up in anticipation of World War II. It was not a union shop in those days.

All week long, we took the work as it came. But on Friday morning, we began a production tactic that was as clever as it was wrong. Orders that could be produced quickly and at a good piece rate were identified and held aside until we heard whether or not we would be working on Saturday. If we weren't asked to work Saturday, we polished off the easy work late Friday afternoon. If we were notified to report Saturday, the high-rate, easy-to-produce stuff got pushed into corners, and the slow work got done first. The reason was simple: We got time and a half for what we did on Saturday, so we saved the high-volume orders until then.

This story makes two points. First, workers take a hand in the planning of work and work hard if they can realize accomplishment. Money, of course, played a part in that experience, but it was still work. The other point is that, where management fails to act, workers tend to take over. And they do it on their own terms. It is that way with both the quality of work and the quantity of work. Management is expected to set standards. When it doesn't, the workers set standards of their own.

I'm always impressed with the way young men and women work in a McDonald's restaurant. They always smile, ask for the order politely, and handle its assembling with alertness. They give quality service at quantity speed. Of course, it's a simple job, and they're backed up by what appears to be a very efficient production operation. They're unlikely to be confronted with unusual requests, and they probably don't encounter many difficulties with customers. But the fact remains that they do their jobs well, cheerfully, and with quality. It says something for young people. It also says something for their management and its attention to detail. That management begins by setting standards, providing good training, and then supervising carefully. Let any one of those necessary management actions slip, and Big Mac slips, too.

Quality and quantity workmanship has to be undergirded with pride in workmanship. Are there proud workers today? I honestly believe there are (witness McDonald's). For many years, Chrysler introduced its new models in the fall. The first to see them were dealers and their salesmen. On the weekend following the dealer show, plant employees were invited to bring their families in and show off the new models. It was fun to watch as the line employees pointed with pride to the part of the automobile they had had something to do with. Work has dignity, work has pride, work is rewarding in ways other than the paycheck. It's the impact manager who keeps employee interest pointed in those directions each working day.

And what about profits? Do workers have a stake or interest in them? The impact manager can make an effective argument for profits that rise out of the labors of those who may not see those profits turn up directly in their paychecks.

Effective managers communicate the fact that they're profitable. They make it clear that profitability is the foundation of job security. They let people know that the enterprise that flourishes is the one that grows, and that growth is the key to promotions, better pay, and benefits. And they show the absolute relationship between quality and quantity and profitability.

Workers expect managers to ask them for a full day's work. They expect to be asked to produce quality products. Even if they haven't studied economics, they know that a company that doesn't turn a profit can't exist forever. Impact managers give people credit for knowing these things, and they manage accordingly—with respect, encouragement, help, firmness, and fairness.

Indeed, what else is a manager for?

Interim Impact Inventory

1. Do you feel that those who buy your product or service are getting what they pay for?

2. Do you feel that you and the people who report to you are making a real contribution to your company's profits?

3. Are your subordinates quality conscious and volume conscious because of your example and instruction?

4. Does your department take pride in achieving, and do you recognize people for achievement?

5. Do your subordinates persist in maintaining quality and volume, even in your absence?

6. Do you involve people in quality and volume planning on a regular basis?

7. Are you openly proud of the fact that you work for a profitable company?

EVERY COIN HAS TWO SIDES

The very purpose of the management role is to vest an individual with the authority to function through others. Along with that authority goes the responsibility for what happens. No manager is worth his salt if he isn't willing to take responsibility. "The buck stops here" should be written on the mind of every manager.

Yet I have seen and worked with managers who were all smiles when everything went along according to plan but were quick to lay blame on a subordinate when it didn't. If the project went right, they took all the credit. If it went wrong, they tried to take none of the blame. This is precisely the opposite of the impact manager's point of view.

The best managers take an adult point of view. They recognize the hazards inherent in leadership. They know that their superiors know that when assignments were made, they included the burden of full responsibility as well as the full reward for achievement. Subordinates know that too. They can help or hinder a manager in carrying out assigned tasks. The effective manager's only hope lies in his willingness to accept responsibility and share credit on a regular, full-time basis.

There's nothing altruistic about such an attitude. It's inescapable. When you don't take that attitude, the only one fooled is yourself. Delusion eats away at relationships, up and down alike, and the manager loses the respect of superiors and subordinates. And where does his support come from then?

The Watergate incident was a classic example of bright managers attempting to lay off blame on someone else. Of course, each thought the other was more guilty than he, but there were few willing to take any blame on themselves. And what happened? Everyone lost. Public opinion came into play. Right or wrong, opinion ruled. That's true in business, too. The farther down the line blame is passed, the more erosive it becomes. Effective managers stop the blame passing before it becomes name calling.

I've watched poorly conceived sales campaigns fail with near predictability. When sales volume failed to materialize, the leader of the sales effort used such excuses as: the weather was bad; the competition made a counterattack; or the sales force didn't function properly. There was hardly a word about the ill-planned campaign, just that everyone else hadn't come through. The net result was even less support the next time around. Finally, the manager became unable to function. Support evaporated from below. When that was recognized, it was also withdrawn from above.

Conversely, I've witnessed successful projects in which the manager could very appropriately have taken full credit. The original idea was his. The planning that went into it bore his mark. Much of the execution of the project involved him directly. Yet, at the conclusion of the successful effort, he called everyone together and pointed out the contribution of each member of the team. His support from below was thereby strengthened, and his support from above became stronger. His willingness to share credit thus generated not only goodwill but good work. That's a true impact manager!

This doesn't mean that, when something goes wrong, the manager assumes all the blame without making subordinates aware of their share of it. A manager is derelict if he doesn't take corrective action. But that's done in another way, perhaps in a counseling session, where things get straightened out for future action. Nor does it mean that the manager doesn't take credit for a successful effort. Remember, when a team wins, its coach is carried from the field.

Shouldering responsibility and sharing credit should begin early in a manager's career. Once he learns that it can be done without a threat to himself, he gathers courage to do more of it. The more he does, the harder it works for him. Best of all, it's simple and honest and readily observable in its impact.

Think of blame and credit from the employee's point of view. In what kind of environment is the best kind of work performed? Have you ever worked in circumstances where you were uptight and threatened, where you moved with a sense of self-protection because attack from above was imminent? Could you give yourself fully to the real work under such circumstances? Did you ever try a new idea or do an old task a new way? Of course not! If it went wrong, you were held up to ridicule; and if it went right, it was ignored.

One of the distinct advantages of a participative management style is that managers and subordinates have the opportunity to discuss projects before they're done. They have a chance to seek some kind of advance approval and share responsibility in advance. They therefore have an advance stake in the credit that accrues to success. It's a case of putting it on a *we* basis: We win together and we lose together. Share and share alike.

Impact managers don't need to grab all the credit, nor do they need the protection of blaming someone else. It's part of their impact pattern, and it's a great pattern to follow.

Interim Impact Inventory

1. Do you acknowledge that the management role has inherent risks just as it has an inherent potential for success?

2. Are you willing to accept the fact that a failure in your department may ultimately result in blame to yourself?

3. Even though you may correct the people who cause a failure, can you also shoulder blame without making excuses or laying it off on subordinates?

4. Do you willingly share credit with subordinates even though the major portion of the project's success was due to your influence and leadership?

5. Do you see your sharing of credit as a motivating factor for the people in your work group?

6. Have you shared credit often enough or specifically enough so that it shows in the attitudes of your subordinates?

7. Do your subordinates suggest innovations with a sense of security against blame, knowing that you will support or guide them?

8. Are your planning sessions open, that is, do participants feel free to make recommendations, and do participants work for the group's success as opposed to working only for themselves?

KEEPING A RISK FROM BEING A GAMBLE

Effective managers understand that there are risks in business, and that taking risks is part of the job. An overly cautious manager often finds himself falling behind a more aggressive competitor. That's particularly true today when so much emphasis is placed on fast-running horses.

But risks need not be gambles. Risks should be calculated, not careless. Whatever managers decide to do, they should see the hazards as well as the objectives. And that leads to careful consideration of fall-back positions or alternatives. Furthermore, risks become less of a gamble when managers can back their actions with the willingness to spend the time and resources it takes to assure success.

Manufacturers generally don't bring new products to market until they have studied the market's potential. If the potential is there, they take the risk of building plants, buying tools, and hiring the manpower required to take advantage of that potential. It's a studied risk, a calculated one, formulated on good research.

Supermarket chains don't build a store and *hope* that traffic will develop. Instead, they study the traffic in that market until they are reasonably certain their new store can enjoy a fair share of business on that site. Risk, to be sure, but preceded by analysis.

Once into the venture, the risk taker has to be willing to support the contention that success is around the corner by going around the corner to meet it. I have yet to see a successful business venture that wasn't accompanied by hard work and cold cash. Strangely enough, some managers don't see it that way.

Reorganizing a department, for instance, has risks. Will new reporting relationships work? Will new procedures required in a new organization work? Will the people work? Will more work be done, or will better work be done? Will this change bring with it the need for still further change? Will facilities be adequate? Will present staff be adequate? Dozens of questions arise in the face of change.

I watched a new manager reorganize a department in the face of what appeared to be rather sticky odds. Most people liked things just as they were. Top management was ambivalent—if it pleased the manager, he could make changes, but there was no particular priority given to changing. Any change was likely to touch off some resistance. Cliques had been formed and alliances made. It was a case of everyone being happy with things as they were but not enough getting done. But in the mind of the manager, the need for change was well worth the risks involved.

The manager's first step was to call in key people for a conference. He asked: "Is there anything we could do better? Is there any way we could do what we're doing better?" The response was hesitant at first. But as time went on, the conference began to yield suggestions.

Then came individual sessions. "In the light of what we discussed yesterday, how do you see your role in this operation? Is there some way you'd like to function that you can't under the current organization?" Again, hesitancy was followed by cooperation.

Minds were already pointed toward change. Resistance was in the wings, but the wisdom of "wait and see" prevailed. Again, key people met in conference over a trial-balloon organization plan. Gains and losses were involved, but there were obvious advantages in the new plan. The preselling had begun.

The change in organization was ultimately accompanied by physical changes in office layout and location. There were new reporting relationships, but few of them came as much of a surprise because careful groundwork had been done by the manager. Many of the people involved rejoiced in the changes. A new beginning and the excitement of challenge faced them. Some grumbled, and some of them were persuaded to accept the change. A few were transferred or released. But the change was made.

It took time, and it took money. It was a risk. But the risk was minimized by the careful expenditure of both time and money and by the proper managing of both.

I have watched manufacturers bring new products to market without backing that risk by spending enough money on advertising and sales promotion. When the products didn't make it, failure was judged to be the fault of design, manufacturing, or the sales organization. Then there's the opposite—a big ad campaign run without ample stock to back it up. Risks require that other risks be taken, or at least they require good sense and the commitment of supportive time and resources.

The manager who is willing to tackle something new and exciting tends to build excitement in those he leads. How dull work life would be if nothing new ever happened! The impact generated by such a manager stimulates more work and better work. Success is doubly rewarded with renewed confidence in decisive leadership.

Interim Impact Inventory

1. Are you willing to take risks in order to achieve certain worthwhile objectives?

2. When you take risks, do you do so with the potential hazards in mind and with alternate courses of action reasonably well formulated?

3. When time permits, do you do careful research to eliminate any suggestion of risk?

4. Are you willing to put extra effort into a project that has a hint of risk with a "the boards are weak, so nail them more carefully" point of view?

5. Do you make clear to your subordinates that the project involves risk and that they will have to pay special attention to it?

6. Have you recognized that the more people become involved in the planning of a project, the better everyone sees potential pitfalls and the harder people work to keep their end up?

7. Are you willing to spend money on a project, even if it cuts into another project or temporarily hurts profitability—assuming, of course, that the payoff is worthwhile?

8. Is your work group stimulated by the prospect of pulling off a new project that others said couldn't be done?

SOME DAYS ARE LIKE THAT

The management role sometimes looks pretty simple. Indeed, a study among workers some years ago revealed that they thought most management people had it pretty easy. Managers, they thought, just sit around and talk. What gets talked about and how it gets talked out, however, can make participants just as physically exhausted as the loading of boxcars. As often as not, the one behind the desk sleeps less well than his critics on the line do.

A classic office one-liner goes, "If you didn't have problems to solve, they wouldn't need you on the job." True, the function of management is to identify and solve problems, to do something better than it is being done now, or to prevent something less good from occurring. No right-thinking manager sees those problems as unpleasant tasks. Instead, they are seen as challenges to ingenuity and perseverance. In fact, solving such problems and seeing beneficial results are the manager's ultimate reward.

When we speak of a manager's willingness to take on unpleasant tasks, we're not referring to the day-to-day handling of business. Under the heading of unpleasant tasks, I'd list such things as layoffs, firings, disciplinary action, fire-fighting actions that disrupt otherwise orderly business, the deletion of a needed program because of a budget cut, and the handling of affairs of a deceased employee. These things happen in the best of businesses. There are managers who take them in stride and some who avoid, postpone, or delegate anything that doesn't suit their taste. True impact managers face up to these unpleasantries, regardless of how they feel about handling them.

A quick comment before going further: Some managers may not see the items I've identified as being unusual, calling them merely day-to-day tasks. If layoffs, firings, disciplinary action, and quick plan changes are commonplace in a business, that business has problems that go deep. And if a manager enjoys doing such tasks he's got problems that are deeper than any I can comment on here.

The manager who is successful with subordinates, peers, and bosses is the manager who steps right up to the unpleasant task and handles it without fuss. My own experience in this has been that, whenever I've postponed or avoided unplesantries, they've always worsened. Handling them clears the air. It also shows those who observe the action that the manager is on top of the job.

I once worked in an organization where one worker routinely took advantage not only of his fellow workers but of his boss, as well. The manager was sensitive and a little apprehensive of the situation. I would guess he might not have felt equal to the verbal barrage he anticipated in return for his disciplinary lecture. At any rate, he postponed taking action sufficiently long enough until others began to take advantage of him. Morale in the organization slipped perilously. Finally, he forced himself to take the necessary action. The troublesome individual's behavior changed, and the organization's morale went back up.

Some years ago, a competent worker under my supervision began to behave erratically. I was not sufficiently attentive at first in noticing the problem because he was extremely clever in concealing it from me. He maintained a fairly good level of productivity but became less and less dependable. He always had what appeared to be valid excuses for being late, leaving early, and missing appointments. Much of his work took him away from the office, and I understood the vagaries of his kind of work, having done it myself for a long time.

His problem was 90 proof, and it had its origins years before I had hired him. Like most alcoholics, he had developed defenses and had enlisted quiet support among his coworkers and other contacts. Others, however, resented him. Word got to me about what was really happening. I didn't relish a confrontation, so there was a period of fretting and fuming without acting.

The sad part was that it was I who suffered, not he. Finally, I began a long string of counseling sessions with him. Each one brought a promise of change. His behavior changed slightly but not totally. After one extremely embarrassing experience, the man had to be fired. I helped him find his next three jobs, but his problem persisted.

A point can be made about the manager's responsibility to prevent negative situations like firings from occurring. Or I could say that a manager should take interim steps to prevent the need for final drastic action. True. But when neither effort by a manager produces fruit, he has to face up to the unpleasantness of taking definite, corrective action. One thing should be noted, however, and that is: The manager who works hard to prevent problems and who does take immediate remedial steps faces final confrontations with greater self-assurance. Equally important, in a disciplinary action, the person disciplined expects it and accepts it.

In discussing the contents of this section with others, I have come upon some bizarre tales. One involved the manager who, when a layoff was ordered, had his secretary notify the affected personnel. Another told of the manager who, when a subordinate was killed in an automobile accident, avoided dealing with it by inventing a trip that called him out of town for three or four days.

Another story told of a manager who, rather than dismiss an employee, arranged a transfer for that person to some not-too-pleasant assignment, the reasoning being that the unwanted worker would quit and the problem would thereby solve itself. He changed his tactics when one subordinate took the transfer, succeeded in turning a bad situation around, became a hero, and later came back as his ex-boss's boss!

Unpleasantness shouldn't be an accepted part of every business day. If it is, as I said earlier, there are deeper problems involved. But when unpleasant tasks do come before the manager, he should confront them with thoughtfulness, care, and authority. Walking away from them, ignoring them in the hope that they'll disappear by themselves, or postponing action in anticipation of a miracle are not the actions of the professional, the impact manager.

Interim Impact Inventory

1. Can you honestly say that such unpleasant duties as firings, reprimands, or other emergency actions are not an everyday occurrence in your operation?

2. Can you recognize situations that require correction early enough to keep them from becoming unpleasant tasks?

3. Do you step up to unpleasant tasks and get them out of your way in a positive manner?

4. Do you make it clear to subordinates who are faced with unpleasant tasks that such situations should be handled as they arise?

5. In the delegation of responsibility, do you pledge your support to those subordinates who have to take disciplinary action
with another worker?

6. Do you keep your pledge to support unpleasant but necessary action?

7. Have you noticed that your reputation for stepping in and
handling things often prevents similar situations from recurring?

THERE'S NOTHING ROSE COLORED
ABOUT BLACK AND WHITE

Effective managers seek the truth. They base their decisions on
facts. They accept realities. When they look at black and white,
they don't wear rose-colored glasses. Or at least that's what we expect them to do.

It's not easy to be objective. Feelings frequently win out over
facts. We are often more sensitive than we are sensible. Then, too,
what is fact to one may not appear to be so to another. We often
perceive the same facts in different ways. Good news to one may
be bad news to someone else. We begin with an attitude or prejudice and see facts in that light. Yet the truly effective manager attempts to use facts as a standard part of his daily work.

In an earlier section, I commented on objectivity versus subjectivity. There's little question about the power of subjectivity—
opinion and point of view. It makes a difference in our lives—in
what we think of people, how they think of us, or what we think
about issues, regardless of the facts involved. This brief discussion
of objectivity accepts the fact that we are highly subjective.

As applied to the manager, objectivity has a number of angles.
First and foremost is the way effective managers begin the approach to decisions and actions. They begin by looking for facts
and gathering data before forming conclusions. This doesn't preclude subjectivity from entering, but it puts subjectivity in perspective. It may all sound quite simple, but it's not hard to find
managers who do just the opposite—who form conclusions first
and then look for facts to support those conclusions. This is probably the single most important flaw in much business judgment

today, and it occurs most frequently in highly authoritative managers.

Look around the average business office today, and you'll see equipment that's not used very often. It may have been purchased when it was thought to be urgently needed, but in reality it was only wanted. Examine a lot of corporate policies and procedures, and you'll find that portions of them were written to satisfy some executive's fancy rather than a business fact or need. Look at some of the products on the market today, and you'll probably discover that what makes them look bad or work improperly was a subjective, last-minute judgment made by an executive who quickly penciled in a change after dozens of designers and engineers had labored for months on the plan's development. "Don't bother me with facts. My mind's already made up!"

Look at some advertising, and you'll recognize that it's aimed at fanning some manager's ego, not at selling merchandise. A look at some stores or offices or factories reveals that the layout was done not for the customer's convenience but for the owner's. The same holds true of much that goes on in government; systems are aimed not at the needs of the people but at the satisfaction of bureaucracy. Lack of objectivity is wasteful. Equally bad is its being noticed and criticized by those who have to work around such foolishness.

I briefly served a client who manufactured a common product needed by everyone. The manufacturing process had at one time been developed personally by the person who was now president of the company. Times changed, tastes changed, costs changed, and similar products were being made differently by competitors. All this innovation provided a cost advantage without noticeable performance loss to the consumer. My client couldn't compete on price, insisted that his quality deserved higher prices, and adamantly refused to change his production methods. Bit by bit, his strong position in the marketplace dwindled, and panic reigned in the sales organization. Finally, the company resorted to dishonest sales and service practices, fell into disrepute, and ultimately went into oblivion. The reason? The president's subjective love affair with his invention.

Lack of objectivity takes its toll in interpersonal relationships, too. Old Charlie is kept in a key job because, in spite of a number of negatives, we think he has clout with important customers. Or we believe he handles well portions of the job that others can't. Or we think dismissing him would cause a demonstration by some of his supporters. I've seen Old Charlies taken out of sensitive positions with never a ripple of opposition from anyone. Those supposedly on his side really hadn't liked him at all. All along, Old Charlie had fooled everyone. Lack of objectivity! Nobody ever took the time to look at the facts.

The more managers discipline themselves to work objectively, the better they can cope with subjectivity. In other words, they discover that facts aren't all bad, that facing them tends to produce better decisions, that facts are defensible and understandable. This doesn't rule out feelings; it merely keeps them from having primary or absolute control.

It's entirely possible to find managers who work so hard at being objective that they never move until *all* the facts are in place. Often, these managers are left at the starting gate. I don't propose this kind of ultracautious management, because it frequently doesn't get anywhere. At times, decisions left to be made until all the facts are on the table are so sterile or stale that they don't stand much chance of coming off well.

My point of view is exemplified best by a system of participative management. Managers who consult with and rely on others to provide input generally emerge with a workable bagful of facts. As inputs are provided by knowledgeable participants, they tend to be tested against the points of view of others. There is time for questioning, time for gut reaction, time for appraisal. Properly done, objectivity is enhanced by such a process.

Effective and objective managers pick up impact value in the respect they earn from those who work with them. Sam always knows where he's going; he never goes off half-cocked. Sue enjoys bringing all the facts into the meeting; she gets everyone thinking along with her. Fred isn't hardheaded, but he's firm minded; he won't take opinions that haven't some basis in fact. Mary's projects always seem to come off pretty much as predicted; there's not a lot of guesswork involved. Managers about whom these things are said are good bets in most businesses. They both look and act like winners.

Subordinates like to go along with a winner. Superiors want winners on their team. If objectivity helps make winners, it should be a part of every manager's tool kit.

Interim Impact Inventory

1. Do you discipline yourself against playing hunches or reacting solely to gut feelings unless there are enough facts in your favor to justify your action?

2. Are your subordinates equally objective in their approach to taking action?

3. Can you call for an action you don't personally appreciate but that factual evidence strongly supports?

4. Will you allow the points of view of others to enter into your judgment, recognizing that opinion may have a real effect on the authority of fact?

5. Do you insist on identifying real problems before taking action on what may be merely a symptom?

6. Can you keep your prejudices from preventing subordinates from doing things which, although correct, may not be done *your* way?

7. Are your business actions taken for the good of the business, as opposed to merely making you feel good or look good?

8. Can subordinates who observe your decision making perceive a pattern of objectivity they can follow?

9. Can you deal with people problems without being blinded by personalities and allegiances?

10. Do you generally work from a position of knowing rather than from one of guessing or hoping?

WHEN FAIR MEANS EXCELLENT

Among the better managers I know, recent legislation on things like equal rights and fair employment practices is considered redundant. Laws that assure equal and proper treatment of employees have been part of their management patterns all along. With these managers, there is no discrimination due to age, sex, race, color, or creed. They just see people who are valuable to the enterprise. To them, the only thing that matters is the work done.

Among the poorer managers I know, the new laws also don't mean much because there are always ways to get around rules. No amount of legislation can make decent, fair human beings of them. They will continue to pursue their prejudices and their pettiness in covert ways. They are bound to lose impact, even with those who tend to be favored by discrimination. The reputation for fairness is a big plus for any manager.

Fairness is an attitude that has to be demonstrated by conscious effort and self-discipline. If a manager isn't concerned with being fair because he feels he is already fair, he may fall short of his goals. In other words, what might have begun as a fair arrangement can deteriorate into an unfair one unless a careful vigil is kept.

Take, for instance, the concept of equal pay for equal work—or its counterpart, which is all too often ignored, equal work for equal pay. A manager hires two people to do the same type of job. One worker displays talents beyond those of his fellow worker. There are therefore times when it's to management's advantage to have these extra skills applied to speed up a project, handle a special order, or favor a special customer. "Get Mary to prepare that report rather than Pete; she handles figures better than he does. Besides, she'll type it up faster." So Mary ends up with more work and not a nickel more pay. Unconscious unfairness!

"There's a meeting in Omaha on Monday morning. Marty is single, Jeff is married. Marty doesn't seem to object to traveling on Sunday afternoon, but Jeff's family needs attention, and Sunday is a family day." Marty gets the assignment to handle the Monday session. And the next time, and the next time. . . .

I've always had a little trouble connecting with the biblical story of the laborers in the vineyard. Just because those who came to work early in the morning contracted for the same rate as those who came to work late in the afternoon doesn't, somehow, erase the discrepancy. Yet time and again, we find ourselves in business situations offering unequal pay for equal work or vice versa. Sometimes it's by design; other times it's a matter of carelessness or ignorance.

Cumbersome as they may often be, personnel wage and salary policies in big corporations are established with the intent of fairness. That is, we work within a wage and salary structure that is supposed to be equal and fair. There are possibilities of inequity here, all of them subject to the decision of the manager, who can move the valued worker up within the parameters of that pay scale on the same regularized basis as the not-so-valuable worker. Merit systems, badly applied, are without merit, especially if a manager is indiscriminate in administering them.

Managers who hide behind automatic pay adjustments are not exercising the judgment for which they are paid. Obviously, many automatic plans were designed to eliminate or minimize oversight of the quiet, mind-your-own-business worker. I have no quarrel with that. But what about the worker who gives a little more than is expected? That worker is held to a routine improvement factor no better than the rest, in spite of the fact that he doesn't deserve to be discriminated against.

In smaller businesses, where formal policies aren't articulated, managers are often free to do what they wish about compensation. I recall counseling with a sales organization that didn't think it at all peculiar that single persons were paid a base salary less than married persons, or that women were compensated at a lower rate than men doing equal work. All this was explained with the argument that turnover was greater among singles and women; it was especially bad among single women. Rubbish! Inverse logic was at work. Wasn't it possible that those who were unfairly treated went elsewhere in search of equity?

Unfairness can be demonstrated in a number of ways. "Give the work to the person who'll do it." "Let's favor this one with overtime; he needs the money." "She's single and probably isn't interested in the promotion; besides, she hasn't complained yet." "Just wink at it when Sam takes an afternoon off, but charge Jerry with a half-day of vacation." Sometimes unfairness is calculated. At other times it's an innocent oversight. Sometimes unfairness is trivial. At other times it's flagrant. In any event, unfairness is noticed by workers, and the manager suffers an impact loss.

Fairness has its hazards, too. Workers who feel that they should be given extra consideration because of longevity or loyalty may feel put out when they don't get it. Here's where management judgment enters. Here's where communications are important. And here's where good policies and procedures explain it all before it happens. It takes nerve to be fair. The effective manager works at it.

Fairness pays off particularly well in long-run dealings with workers, even though it's sometimes difficult to wait for the payoff. One manager I knew and respected found himself in a difficult union negotiation. He had never been soft, was always a stickler for good effort and careful workmanship; but he had always tried to be fair. Now he faced a situation where, out of a sense of fairness, he wanted a temporary easement of one clause in the contract.

The union committee caucused and came back with its approval. And it added one comment that was especially rewarding for the manager: "We wouldn't have given the time to discuss this to most of the people we deal with. But you've always been fair with us, and we think you're trying to be fair in this matter. We'll go along with your request, because we know you wouldn't have made it if you didn't really feel it was the best thing to do in these circumstances."

Fairness, like beauty, is often in the eye of the beholder. A manager doesn't establish a reputation for a fair attitude until he has demonstrated fairness over a long period of time and unless he has taken steps to explain his point of view. Further, a single demonstration of *un*fairness can nullify a good track record for fairness on a long-term basis. That also goes for the innocent unfair act as well as the one that's intentional.

I think it was at General Electric that the phrase "in the balanced best interests of all concerned" was first used with respect to employee rights and benefits. This phrase says it all, and it should be pasted into the hat of every manager who expects to build impact.

Interim Impact Inventory

1. Do you believe in equal opportunity—even without legislation—ignoring such things as age, color, race, and sex?

2. Do you insist on equal distribution of work among subordinates who are in equal pay grades?

3. Do you use pay scales with ample consideration of merit as opposed to a mechanical adherence to them?

4. Are people under your supervision aware that you recommend special rewards for special accomplishments?

5. Is fairness ever a topic of conversation at your staff meetings—not as a matter of show, but as applied to a specific situation?

6. From time to time, do you take a reading on your attempts to be fair and the actual results of your actions?

7. Would you say that, in the eyes of those with whom you associate (superiors, peers, and subordinates) you are considered a fair person?

A SYMBIOTIC SYNERGISM

Two definitions: *symbiosis*—two dissimilar organisms living in a mutually beneficial relationship; *synergism*—cooperative action such that the total effect is greater than the sum of the effects taken independently. Now let's look at these dictionary definitions in plain English.

Two very important attitudes that add impact to managers and help them operate effectively are a sense of loyalty and a concern for others. Although similar, they are not the same; but they deserve to be discussed together. They are attitudes that help weld an organization together and make it function with advantage to everyone (symbiosis) and with specific advantage to the company.

Managers who can generate loyalty get work groups to produce as a group, not merely as a collection of individuals. Such managers recognize that the yield of the group exceeds the cumulative yield of individuals (synergism). They also realize that, without loyalties to the group, the company, the manager, and each other, there is a subtractive effect. Each person makes his own way, frequently achieving at the expense of others but ultimately at the group's expense. There has to be a sense of the team without complete sacrifice of the sense of the individual.

There are blind loyalties—"My country, right or wrong," "My company, right or wrong." They serve on a short-term basis, but they don't prevent on an extended basis such problems as lethargy, turnover of personnel, cheating, and lack of cooperation. If a manager can develop loyalties only in the short run, he's not doing himself or others much good. There are enough people who reject such loyalties, and with considerable justification.

Then there are loyalties that are informed, studied, deserved, and based on reality. These loyalties are largely the result of a manager's attitude—repeatedly demonstrated. And such loyalties are multidirectional; they go up, down, and laterally. "I am loyal, you are loyal, we are loyal, they are loyal." It's almost like conjugating a verb.

Without loyalties that include the company, the manager, and fellow workers, it's possible to come up with the following kind of situation—one that prevails in a sales organization with which I'm familiar. The sales manager gives his salesmen (all of whom are on commission) a pep talk: "You make it on your own. Be aggressive.

Beat out the next guy. Only winners are wanted on this team."
And that's precisely the way they sell. Nobody covers for anyone
else. Everybody tries to steal the other guy's deals. Customers are
pressured mercilessly. And the organization is known as a band of
pirates. Turnover is awesome, but the manager thinks that's fine.
A revolving door means survival of the fittest; since new salesmen
are always hungry, they are expected to work harder.

The opposite is true in another sales organization I know of. The
sales force has a sense of permanence. A prearranged cover system
exists. Sales personnel are supported by the manager, who has
created a bonus pot from the commissions on house deals. This
builds the type of competitiveness that gets individual salespeople
to work toward their own objectives rather than against each other.
These salesmen are steeped in the concept that as the business
prospers, they prosper, and vice versa. And they do prosper,
thanks to the loyal attitude that originates with their leadership.

Some of the finest loyalty I've ever witnessed came in situations
that really tested loyalty. ("And there came down one day a decree
from Caesar Augustus . . .") As one particular order trickled down
through the organization, it met a good deal of resistance. One
manager midway down the line admitted to his work group that
he, too, had reservations about the project and had voiced his opposition. "But," he said, "the people upstairs may see things in
this that you and I don't. We'll never know whether they're right
or wrong unless we give it a try. Only if we fail when doing it their
way will we know how right we are. They're too far into this project to back off now. But because they respect our judgment,
they've conceded to making running changes if we run into real
snags. I told Phil that if anyone could make this work, this department could. So let's give it an honest try." This was loyalty of a
sensible sort; it elicited an effort that was supportive rather than
reluctant and contrary.

Managers can't expect the loyalty-up attitude to prevail if it's not
appropriately balanced with loyalty-down. Impact managers stand
up for the people in their organizations, give them deserved
credit, keep them from some of the hassles that can cause problems. They realize that work is accomplished best when it's evident that those involved enjoy mutually beneficial relationships.
Then the manager has a functioning team that accomplishes more
than its individual members could achieve separately.

This brings up the second significant attitude—concern for the welfare and progress of others. Don't think of it as being patriarchal but rather as sensibly reciprocal. It means that what benefits me benefits the people in this department; what benefits those people benefits me. Strangely, this is not well understood by many managers, and the misunderstanding works unseen to their disadvantage.

Some years back, I worked close to an organization operated by a very brass-tacks manager. He prided himself on giving no quarter to those in his work group. I must admit that he gave himself few privileges, either; but there were occasions when that, also, was seen as stupid by all concerned. On the morning of a very important meeting, one of his subordinates came to him with a personal request—his wife had become ill, and the doctor felt she should be taken to the hospital. Could he skip the afternoon portion of the meeting?

The employee wasn't scheduled to be an active participant that afternoon. Indeed, he had made his presentation in the morning under considerable emotional strain. Imagine how he felt when he was told, "Have her call a cab. The meeting will be over at five, and you'll be able to get there for evening visiting hours."

Another time, another manager, another meeting: An out-of-town trip was considered important but not vital. It was possible either to reschedule it or settle the matter without requiring a trip by the affected party. The manager insisted that the person go, even though he was aware that one of the evenings away was the night of the traveler's son's high-school commencement. It was, I believe, the same manager who called a special Saturday morning meeting and dragged it out until 1:00 P.M., even though he was well aware that one of his subordinates had a daughter who was to be married that afternoon at 2:30 P.M., some 25 miles away.

Justice sometimes prevails, but not always. The managers in each instance cited had had relatively meteoric rises in their respective organizations, only to be pushed out of the company later on. Their complete disregard for the welfare of others ultimately resulted in an impact loss with their subordinates, who found interesting ways to undermine their boss's progress. When a manager can't manage because his subordinates won't let him, his superiors sooner or later find ways of setting *him* aside.

A generous manager of my acquaintance once confided in me:

"You know, every year we discuss and review salaries in each department. Several years in a row, Harry rated his people fairly well but recommended marginal salary improvements for them. When I saw his people lagging behind others in the company, I drew him out on the subject. He told me that it was just another demonstration of his careful management in cost effectiveness, and that his workers hadn't seemed to complain. I didn't tell him he was wrong. But when he got his raise from me that year, it was about half of what he expected. It didn't take long for Harry to complain. I told him he had taught me a great lesson in expense control, and that if he hadn't complained, I'd have left it at that. We made an adjustment in Harry's salary, but only after he had gone over some of his workers' pay programs. I have no intention of giving this company away, but neither will I be guilty of stealing it back from the people who make it."

When people have personal problems, managers should realize that, until those problems are resolved, they won't work at 100 percent. Illness, trouble at home, discomfort, or a lack of safety in the work environment—any distraction from the work is a matter worthy of attention by the manager.

Then there's the manager who is so pleased with his own organization that losing a member of the group is sheer agony. When asked if one of the workers is available for promotion to another department, he finds reasons why it can't be done. When Sylvia overhears in the washroom that she was considered for promotion but wasn't "available," with what kind of work attitude does she return to her desk?

One of my all-time favorite managers once told me that promotions out of his department were his best advertising. "When word gets around that all these good people came from my organization, other good people want to work here. And when people make good after a start here, they tell others how great this department is. Developing people for other departments isn't necessarily an unselfish action. Heck, no! In the final analysis, it makes my work a lot easier as a result of the cooperation I get from other departments to which those good employees go. A number of my own promotions have come because of that attitude."

Loyalty demonstrated. Concern for the welfare and progress of others. Neither of these is altruistic when we consider that it brings about a healthy group attitude and a responsive feeling for the manager that's bound to pay off for everyone. The happiest managers I know are those who have this attitude. They may not consciously express the results as a symbiotic synergism, but that's what they have at their plant or office.

Interim Impact Inventory

1. Can you honestly say that your organization is a unit, that it works toward common goals and firmly accepts you as the leader?

2. Will people in your work group tackle certain projects out of a sense of loyalty, even though, had they been given a voice in deciding, they might have done it differently?

3. When the occasion arises, do you defend your group against others, and does your group know about it?

4. Are you considerate of individuals in your organization in the same way you expect them to be considerate of you and the organization itself?

5. Will subordinates cover for each other in an emergency, even if it means adding to their own workload?

6. Do you seek outside opportunities for valued members of your work group, even if the loss of those people puts a burden on you for the time being?

7. If you left the work group tomorrow, would the group sincerely lament your leaving, and would its members demonstrate their feelings to you?

8. If you are absent for any reason, does the work go on with a high level of effectiveness and without internal friction?

Part 5
Negatives That Dilute Impact and Are Worth Watching

IT ALL ADDS UP TO EFFECTIVENESS

Our discussion of impact managers began with the premise that managers are measured not only by what they do but by how they do it. It should be obvious by now that managerial style is what puts the real edge on productivity. The more style and the better the style is applied, the greater are the results.

We began with a person with knowledge and skill, someone who knows what the job's all about and understands the organization and how to function within it. This manager knows how to organize work and put people at it. He knows how to communicate. He has the kind of general business knowledge and sense that makes him capable of understanding conditions surrounding his business and the people who come in contact with it. In short, we began with a functional, business-oriented human being capable of suitable performance.

To that we added consideration of the personal qualities that made him capable of impressing people and connecting with them. If a manager's work is performed through other people, it follows that he will work better if their feelings about him are positive. Therefore, how he looks and projects himself into the minds of his subordinates has a lot to do with how well he will lead them in the work to be done. But that's not all. He also has to be able to keep abreast of what's going on, to translate knowledge into decisions, instructions, action, and results. Among other desirable qualities, this takes a lot of patience, creativity, and integrity. He is not only a pleasant person to be around, but a positive person with definite goals and a plan to achieve them.

Finally, attitudes revealed by a manager's behavior came into play. Self-confidence, ambition, and determination are important; they are reflected in responses of the workforce. He expresses concern for quality, volume, and profitability. He's businesslike, and other people know it. He's willing to take on responsibility, share credit, take reasonable risks, and spend the time, money, and energy needed to get the job done. When things don't go well, he can take it. He's objective, tries to be fair, and generates a sense of loyalty as he demonstrates an honest concern for the welfare and progress of the people with whom he comes in contact. He's a worker who expects others to work. He's a human being who sees others as human beings. He's a person who leads people into accomplishments; he doesn't just send them off to run errands.

At the outset, I confessed that the arithmetic in the rating scale might be wrong. But I held that the important thing to see is the relationships between the impact points earned as the result of fulfilling as many of these requirements as possible. If a manager rated, say, 65 in knowledge and skill, picked up 20 of the 30 available points for personal qualities, and managed to score another 20 to 25 points for attitude, he came out above our arbitrary 100-point level of acceptance. Such a manager is probably reasonably effective and properly placed among the average of managers at work today.

A superior manager would have picked up about 70 points for knowledge and skill, added 24 to 26 points for personal qualities, and another 24 to 26 points for attitude, which add up to about 120, for a healthy rating. Not many managers can win all the points in all classifications. At least, I've met few who could do it, and it would take someone more observant than I to do the rating.

These ratings were created subjectively. People will look at them subjectively, and evaluations with them will be made subjectively. As we said earlier, that's pretty much how people who work daily under supervision look at their managers.

Now let's look at some other factors. Again, they are admittedly subjective. These are the ones that tend to rob managers of impact. In the next few pages, I will describe some characteristics that cause many managers a great deal of difficulty.

"THERE'S ONE THING I DON'T LIKE . . . OR TWO . . . OR THREE"

Nobody's perfect. What's worse, some are less perfect than others.

As a class, managers seem to have a few failings that are fairly exclusive to them. That is, they work and live in circumstances in which otherwise normal personal characteristics go out of control and actually work against them. If these characteristics are not exclusive at the management level, at least they are more observable at that level. In some cases, it must be admitted, these characteristics can play out best (or worst) as the level goes up. In other words, who else but the boss could do these things and actually get away with them?

Some of the negative impact characteristics in managers are actually positive characteristics that are badly understood, poorly applied, or out of control. Arrogance, for instance. This characteristic may often be a badly demonstrated case of self-confidence. Or vindictiveness. Could this be a misapplied sense of justice? Let's look briefly at some characteristics that occasionally develop even in very good managers, often without their recognizing what is happening.

Arrogance

This quality reveals itself in many ways. Sometimes it's a matter of physical bearing, where posture signals a feeling of superiority or a swagger that suggests an attitude of supremacy. It can be a smirk on the face when someone else is talking, or it can be ignoring other people's presence by just not looking at them or not responding to what is being said. Arrogance is the unreturned phone call, the unanswered memo—projecting the attitude that "people come to me."

Arrogance can be vocal, too. It's the sarcastic remark that denigrates another's point of view. In this regard, it's often passed off as humor, which is a dangerous way to be funny. Arrogance can be the disregarding of another's point of view without acknowledgment or explanation. And it can be seen in the manager who never solicits another point of view. "All decisions are mine, and my judgment is supreme."

Arrogance is a disease particularly endemic to the young executive. Arrogance is the mistaken notion that if the manager has come so far so fast, he must have some inexplicable talent that's responsible for his speedy ascent. Arrogance says: "This is my department. They are my people. It is my achievement. I did all this." The manager who persists in this kind of arrogance soon discovers he has no department, no people, and that it is hard to come by achievement without them.

An arrogant manager lends himself poorly to the participative management style. To be sure, he does call meetings, but only to give orders, establish his priority, and exult in applause. He may think he is taking the participative approach and that he listens to counsel, but his conferences generally sound otherwise: "I've decided to do this, and I'd like your reaction, Bill (or Jack or Laura or Jim)." This is management by consensus or endorsement, and only the strong can resist it.

I know a manager who has done hundreds of other managers a favor. He is well respected, kindly, circumspect, and so well fortified in his position that he dares intervene when he feels the occasion requires it. From time to time, he calls in young managers who are not under his direct supervision and tells them they've done very well, that they have moved ahead in a very positive manner. But he also tells them about a few little problems appearing on the horizon that could prevent their further sucess. "Word is getting around that you're behaving as if you're wiser than God Himself." The truly wise listen and change their routines. Others discover later that they should have.

Vindictiveness

"I'll get you sometime, you. . . ." Managers who think this way often receive the same kind of treatment in return. "Getting back"—the expression suggests that the street goes two ways. Yet vindictiveness is the mark of many managers, unfortunately some of whom are highly placed.

The vindictive manager is a coward. He nods approval, then lies in wait for a chance to fight back. Vindictiveness generally doesn't right a wrong, but it does usually wrong a right. If vindictive people can't fight back and win, they wait and undermine.

Vindictiveness can go both up and down the ladder. Vindictive managers undermine other managers and they undermine their subordinates. But it must also be remembered that their subordinates often have the last word; they find ways to make the manager's work more difficult or less effective. That's where the most negative kind of impact comes from.

I recall being the butt of a manager's vindictiveness very early in my work life. I was working in a factory at a job that was just a touch less dirty than some others in the shop. The straw boss came along one day, soliciting for a community charity. As a school kid, I had given a dime or a quarter to the cause for several years. Now that I was being asked to give generously, I signed up for three dollars. I was quite satisfied that I was doing a lot, if you consider my average weekly pay was only $26.

A half-hour later, the straw boss came back and told me that the foreman said I had to give five dollars. I don't know where I acquired my sudden bravery, but I said that three was what I had offered, and three was all they would get. I was called into the foreman's office. "I understand you refused to give to charity," he said. "No, sir," I replied. "I just refused to be told how much to give." I then proceeded to tell him that my parents had struggled through the Depression and that I was trying to help at home. He nodded, excused me, and I thought the matter had been settled.

Two weeks later, I was transferred to a very dirty job with no overtime. I worked at that job for three or four weeks, taking home an average of about $16 a week. A month later, I was told that they needed me back on my original job. It was only then that the matter was settled. I had learned that standing my ground had not been worth the two dollars, that management had a way to let me know who was boss. Vindictiveness is the silent weapon of the cowardly boss.

Those were the Dark Ages. That doesn't happen today. Or does it? Two young managers are vying for the same promotion. Paul is chosen over Jack, and Jack's jealousy is evident. Their paths separate widely for several years. Jack's career flourishes even better than that of Paul, the man who earlier beat him out. Ten years later, they meet again, this time in a line-staff relationship in which Jack is the ranking man. Paul, however, has become an expert in his staff job, and it is his responsibility to provide operating counsel to Jack.

Jack won't take Paul's advice, won't accept his good-natured offers to take on certain jobs, and actually begins a campaign to undermine Paul's reputation with top management. He engineers a transfer for Paul into a job that appears to have little potential, a little-known research operation that has something to do with energy conservation. The Arab oil embargo puts Paul into the corporate spotlight, much to Jack's chagrin.

How different is the story my son Jim tells of his experience in Vietnam. A college graduate with a start on graduate work, he had chosen not to go for a commission. Instead, he took his chances with the troops. He arrived in Vietnam as a sergeant and was assigned to the 101st Airborne Division. One day a captain approached him and asked, "What's a kid like you doing in a place like this?" The ensuing conversation resulted in Jim's being selected to manage a parts depot in a forward area. He was familiar with the business, so it was a good assignment. At least, he wasn't slogging around in the jungles anymore. His mother and I were much relieved.

About two weeks after taking on the new job, he and others doing similar work were called together for special instruction on a new procedure to be followed. A general of some importance gave the lecture. At the end of his presentation, the general asked if there were any questions or comments. Of course, when generals ask that question, they are merely extending a courtesy and don't expect a response.

But this general got one. A young sergeant with two weeks on the new job said, "Sir, I think there's a simpler way to do that." (How stupid this younger generation!) The general asked the sergeant how he would go about it. To make a long story short, Jim began his explanation. What he said seemed to make sense to the general who asked him to come forward and put the procedure on the chalkboard. When the task was done, the general turned to the group and said, "I agree with this young man. Forget what I told you to do. Remember and do what you see here on the board. *Now* are there any questions the sergeant or I can answer?"

That sergeant was my son, and I half expected to get a letter a week later telling me he was back in the jungle. It would have been an easy matter to arrange. But the general was an impact manager whose rank was too high to be threatened and who was too big to indulge in the pettiness of vindictive action. He was a manager who earned impact, because he wasn't afraid to lose it!

Recklessness

There's a premium placed on action in business. We like to see things happen. The manager who gets an activity going and shows results is given kudos. We give him points for self-confidence, ambition, determination, decisiveness, and a willingness to take risks. We also keep score on the results and the costs involved in achieving those results.

A reckless manager pushes the good qualities of his management style beyond approval. He develops a reputation for winning big—also a reputation for losing big. His subordinates are frequently uneasy about following him. His superiors become concerned about giving approval to his projects.

Recklessness is typified by poor planning and scanty research.

It's the mark of the hunch player and the go-for-broke bettor. The reckless manager runs faster than his organization; he leaves it to others to pick up the pieces. Two wins in a row make him a hero, but two losses in a row make him a bum.

Reckless managers tend to be poor team players; they seldom take counsel and often don't line up an organization carefully enough to handle the action. The people under them work at a disadvantage—not enough time, not enough ready resources, not enough manpower, not enough assurance that what they're doing will work. Their motivation is shaky. Do it well, and you'll be called on to do it again and again. Do it poorly, and you'll be blamed for the failure.

The manager who works in a participative style may still move with vigor and may still take risks, but the involvement of others in preplanning helps erase the uneasiness while, at the same time, it broadens the base of understanding and the range of cooperation. It's possible to have excitement without danger and to have progress without pain.

Selfishness

We begin this way. It's natural and defensible. St. Thomas Aquinas said that the Christian life is one of enlightened selfishness. Note the word "enlightened."

There's nothing wrong with wanting to do well for ourselves. But to want to do well exclusively for ourselves is another matter. To be sure, we should take care of Number One, but can we afford to do it at the expense of Two and Three? The enlightened manager knows he can't be selfish and continue to get the cooperation of those who witness his selfishness.

I once worked in an enterprise that was occasionally only marginally profitable. From time to time, there came a year when everything fell into place nicely, and the books showed a healthy gain. When that happened, the owner insisted on distributing most of the profits among his workers. I suggested that, perhaps, he might want to retain more of the earnings—a move I still believe would have enhanced the health of the operation and would have made day-to-day management simpler. But the man's reasoning was simple and direct: "The people made that profit. They know when it has been a good year and when it has been a bad one. They can remember some long, hard days of work and worry that were necessary to pull off our achievements. This way they can equate effort with earnings. They get a nice feeling about that—and so do I."

A lot of managers wouldn't do that. Nor do they share with others information that might help them do the job better. Nor would they share credit opportunities or good working conditions. Their workers ply their trades in dirty corners while the boss's office rivals the Taj Mahal. They neglect to recognize that giving a little can result in getting a lot.

I work in an industry where sales contests are common. Quite often winners receive a nice trip. There's a definite correlation between the successful sales organization and the sales manager or owner who occasionally turns the tickets he wins over to an outstanding salesman with the comment, "I won it, but you earned it." This is quite the opposite of another organization I was associated with where sales premiums were kept secret from the sales force, and the boss kept the prizes for himself.

The old cliché, "The harder I worked, the luckier I got," has its counterpart in the one that says, "The more I gave, the more I got." There are a few managers who haven't discovered either of those truths.

Laziness

We expect that those who become managers are what the behaviorists label "achievers." It's an understandable assumption, but it's not always a true one. There are many managers who, after years of commendable exertion, suddenly decide they can now start to sit it out. Unfortunately, their laziness becomes contagious.

The manager who creates a sinecure for himself may also create for himself a regressive work organization. Creative and ambitious people shy away from such situations, because they spell dead end. Organizations that don't attempt new projects or take on exciting challenges don't attract good people. However comfortable the situation may be, achievement—the real satisfier, according to Herzberg—isn't to be had in such cases.

Someone once said, "Getting there isn't half the fun. It's all the fun!" Truly successful managers—even those who are on a career plateau—work at their jobs and get others to work at theirs as though their very lives depended upon it. How right that is. They do!

Permissiveness

Some observers equate permissiveness with laziness. Yet there are some very active managers who become quite permissive. They are managers by exception: "If it's going fairly well, let it go." Sometimes they see an aspect of their business as having little or no priority, so they let Sam handle it the best he can.

Permissiveness invites several problems, not the least of them an employee attitude of: "If the boss doesn't care, why should I?" Consequently, what was handled indifferently before doesn't get handled at all now. Permissiveness also invites the usurping of authority, stealing, and cheating, and ultimately leads to disregard and disrespect for the leadership.

Permissiveness doesn't mean passing off a responsibility to a subordinate with a clear understanding of what is to be done. Nor is it a matter of calling Mike in and asking him how he intends to get something done, then letting him do it. Those are examples of participative management. Permissive management just hopes that someone will recognize the need to do something and will do it sometime, somehow.

Oddly enough, highly directive managers are often guilty of permissive management. They're so busy bossing some parts of their enterprise that they just have to overlook others. Sometimes they take on a pose of charitableness to give the impression of allowing a sense of freedom. In any case, permissive management is no management at all. The manager who regularly shrugs off a part of his responsibility in this way is headed for trouble. Subordinates feel this weakness and superiors see it. He is robbed of impact from all sides.

The above six negative management traits can rob you of many impact points. Some of them aren't easily unlearned, but the serious manager makes an honest attempt not to let any of them surface to a measurable degree. In the following chapter, we'll take up several more.

Interim Impact Inventory

1. Do you guard against any show of superiority—the quick put-down, the biting remark, the ignoring of subordinates, or the reminder to others of how important you are?

2. Do you watch the reactions of others to see whether or not anything you might have said or done was offensive to them?

3. Do you solicit opinions from others, and do you acknowledge such contributions with sincerity?

4. Can you leave a disagreeable matter as being over without harboring a grudge or plotting retribution?

5. Can you publicly concede a point to another without maneuvering to come out on top in some other way?

6. Do you consider the risks of all the projects you undertake—risks that might jeopardize the safety and well-being of others in the enterprise?

7. Are you willing to share your time, information, expertise, resources, credit, and approval with others?

8. Would your subordinates readily admit that you are probably as hard working as anyone else?

9. Do you attempt to keep up to date on all phases of your operation, even the less visible ones, so that everyone is conscious of your attention and concern?

10. Do your subordinates have reason to work hard for you because you demonstrate your interest and pride in them?

ADDING TO THE MINUSES

Here are several more traits, tendencies, and attitudes that some managers employ to their detriment. Those who are guilty seldom confess it, because (a) they're unconscious of their negative behavior, or (b) they think it's their prerogative as managers to operate in these ways.

Abrasiveness

A quick check of Roget's Thesaurus gives us quite a few words related to abrasion: pulverize, granulate, scrape, file, abrade, grind, grate, pound, bruise, crunch, crumble, disintegrate. A quick question: How would you like any of these to happen to you? Better yet, if you were subjected to such conditions, is it likely that you'd be productive?

Some managers demonstrate their superiority by taking an abrasive attitude toward those who work under their supervision. "Get me that memo from the file." "Type this up in a hurry." "Pick up

Irwin at the airport." "Who told you to do it that way?" "Get out of my way." "That's dumb." "I might have known it wouldn't come out right if you did it." Picture all these nice instructions and admonitions uttered with a grunt or a growl.

People will get the memo from the file, type up things in a hurry, pick up someone at the airport, and so on. They'll take correction and criticism, too. Getting people to do things is always possible. But getting them to do things willingly or cheerfully is another matter.

Abrasive managers should listen to themselves. They're generally high achievers who want to take the shortest way. They wonder why their turnover of personnel is so great, why people take all the sick days allowed in the contract, or why the place falls apart when they're away. It's simple. People who are rubbed hard become pretty smooth at finding ways to avoid not only the boss but the work he has for them.

Intemperance

Too much of anything can cause problems. Common areas of intemperance: He drinks too much, eats too much, plays too hard, works too long (and so forth). Of course, if any of these get in a manager's way, it's possible they can subtract from his effectiveness. The alcoholic and the workaholic alike can ruin productive relationships.

In this context intemperance refers to misdirected or uncontrolled speech or action met from time to time in business situations. "The boss is upset and he's throwing a fit" is the kind of intemperance that blows your top but also blows your opportunity to be constructive in a managerial role. Mark Twain once said about being angry that you should count to four, then swear very hard. Some managers never get to three.

Impassioned outbursts generally draw passionate responses or result in hasty withdrawals. In either case, not much good results. I sat in a manager's office one morning and listened to one end of a telephone call in which directive and invective were so badly mixed that I wondered whether the individual at the other end could distinguish between the two. To top it off, when the call was concluded, the offender turned to me and beamed, "I guess he got the message. He found out who he was talking to." Yes, indeed, he got the message that he was talking to an undisciplined boor who will get operation without *co*operation.

There are times when we go at it head to head in business. And there are times when tempers flare and expression becomes heated. However, the manager who routinely loses his temper loses not only his poise but his punch as well. He shows himself to be both not in command of himself and incapable of being in full command of his work group.

I have sat across the desk from managers who disagreed with me, were critical of something I had done or not done, and were in a position to put me away in fine style. I understood them very well as they spoke in firm, deliberate tones and in words that were relevant and socially acceptable. More important, however, is that I walked away from such encounters with the determination to do something *for* them rather than something *to* them.

That's particularly important in a tough neighborhood!

Impetuousness

The winner is the runner who gets there first. The active manager generally eclipses the careful, methodical planner. That's pretty much the way it is. But the manager who beats both of them to the finish line is the one who can quickly think through a course of action and take it to an acceptable result.

Impetuous managers are those who pull the trigger before they draw the gun. They're the ones who move quickly to solve one problem before they realize that, by doing so, they are creating another one. They commit resources they don't have. They run into snags that require overtime, dislocation of other projects, inconvenience, and added cost. Their workers are often doing something before they know *what* they're doing. Consequently, they work under the handicaps of ignorance, confusion, and uncertainty.

There's a difference between the impetuous manager and the one who is able to turn on a dime and go in a new direction because he has provisional plans and backup resources to employ. Subordinates admire the latter because they know he has anticipated fast action. Here, again, the participative manager has readied his people for optional routes of action. They're in on it from the beginning and are ready to go when the bell rings.

Failure of a precipitate action generally gets passed off onto some poor soul down the organization ladder who couldn't move fast enough. Impetuous managers are equally quick with reprimands. Or their actions result in cover-ups: "We just don't want people to know this or remember it." This kind of avoidance can survive only so long. Enough minor failures equal one major failure.

Some managers are masters of hasty action. Some, indeed, create their own crises so that they can demonstrate their quick responses. Good top management keeps its eyes open for these quick actors. When the instant hero is applauded, he is the perfect exemplar of the Peter Principle; given the opportunity, he'll rise to his own level of incompetence. Then comes the weeding-out process. When you tear out big weeds, it's terribly hard on the lawn.

Impact managers know the difference between fast, incisive, and planned action and the quick-on-the-trigger-but-slow-on-the-draw kind of action that more often than not aborts. Their subordinates know it, too. They help the manager bring off programs to successful conclusions. And word reaches the top floor pretty fast as well.

Uniqueness

A better way to restate uniqueness is "too different." We're intrigued by those who are unusual in appearance, style, or personality, but somehow we can't connect with those who are so different they don't fit.

There are many such people in the business world these days. There's the aspiring manager who insists on expressing his own lifestyle by wearing clothes that don't fit the office in which he works. He'll continue to aspire, but he won't make it. There's the would-be manager who writes memos and reports to fit his own format rather than the standards of the corporation. Wait until one of his epistles reaches the top floor attached to a cover letter from his boss. There's the individual who insists that his office be informal and decorates it with unusual pictures and mementos. He may be a brilliant engineer or marketing analyst, but he'll have tough going unless his inventions or forecasts are equally unusual—and very workable.

People should be themselves, but they shouldn't expect a company to change its concepts to fit their own. Different, yes; *too* different, no. The manager who wants recognition is well advised to gain it by doing unusual things that bring about desirable unusual results, not just being so different that people stop and gaze.

In saying this, it is not my intention to exclude the manager who seeks change and tries hard to bring it about in an orderly manner. Industry needs such managers. The wiser among them do it within the framework of the understanding of people who couldn't be different if they tried.

Possessiveness

Managers should take an interest, even a proprietary interest, in their work as well as in the people who work with them and the resources allotted to them. However, the mere fact that a worker is on the payroll doesn't mean that worker is the manager's property. There's a limit to the meaning of *my* staff, *my* department, *my* equipment, or *my* project.

Some managers wear a paternal or maternal cloak when it comes to the workforce they supervise. They may be well intentioned regarding the personal lives of their employees, but they are assuming a touch more than they're entitled to when they pry into individual private lives. It's good business to be interested, bad business to take over and advise.

It's fine to consider yourself the custodian of the enterprise, but there are managers who insist on all things being locked and having the key in their pocket. The manager's own files, yes; but the general files, no. If you can't trust your employees, it's unlikely that they'll trust you. I have yet to be betrayed by a fellow worker in whom I placed a confidence. Perhaps it's been just good fortune, but I'd prefer to call it careful selection and good counseling. I learned my lessons from observing some of the greatest managers in the world.

There's good sense in protocol and lines of reporting. However, some managers insist that anyone from the outside must be cleared through them before having access to other people in the department. Imagine how much managerial time is spent in protecting such a point of view. Good managers develop good subordinates who can operate with independence and assume the responsibility of keeping the boss informed.

Possessive managers suffocate an organization when, indeed, they should be ventilating it. The manager who is possessive may think he's protecting his people, his department, and his company, but in fact he's keeping them from doing all they can in his support. Impact managers trust, let go, and show interest, but they don't take over. As they grow in their understanding of participative techniques, it becomes *our* staff, *our* department, *our* project. It's more fun to work with your friends than it is to work under your father.

Unwillingness to Take or Share Blame

Earlier, I extolled the virtues of the manager who is willing to take responsibility and share credit. Not much more need be said on the positive aspects of the subject. It's brought up here in the minus column simply to emphasize its importance.

The participative manager is committed to taking blame when it's deserved, because his decisions are made in the presence of others or as a result of other people's input (this doesn't excuse poor performance by an individual or a group). Properly administered, participative action seats responsibility where it belongs and judges it accordingly. If it doesn't go right, everyone knows where it went wrong.

Impact managers are too big and too strong to push off blame when they're cornered. The blamer or the excuser always reminds me of myself when I make a bad golf shot. My ball may come off the club exceptionally well, but when it hits a tree, my first comment is that the tree spoiled a perfectly good shot. That's nonsense. The tree was there all the time, and I hit my ball into it. It is the same way with those who observe a manager who has to lay off blame. People don't like to work for such a boss, and they don't for long.

Favoritism

One person *always* gets the good assignments. One person *always* gets excused from the dirty work. One person *always* gets the biggest raise. One person *always* gets the opportunity for advancement. In some business organizations, this litany is all too true.

There is generally a reason behind this favoritism. The person so favored has found a way to get to the boss. Undoubtedly, an obligation has been created that has to be met. My caution to the manager is simple: Avoid being obligated; then, no favor has to be returned. The problem is not the closeness that's created between employee and boss, but the separation that's generated between the boss and others. Disguise it all you will, it will still show.

The Green Bay Packers under Vince Lombardi used to say of their coach, "He treats us all the same—lousy." In some respects it's probably safer to do that than show partisanship to one or two individuals. That's because, even if most people are treated well in an organization, the few who are treated with special favor make the others feel ill treated. We tend to skip from good to bad with no stop at all on neutral. If you favor one and leave out nine, the odds are nine to one against the manager.

Again, the participative technique allows managers to show favor wherever it is merited. Best of all, it's in the open for all to see. It's better to have people say, "I can see how the boss gives Wilson such attention. Wilson has good ideas and expresses them well," than to have people say, "How come Wilson gets all the attention? He must know where the body's buried."

Impact managers pay attention to everyone and give opportunities to those who deserve them. They seldom have to defend themselves against unjust criticism for favoritism.

Isolationism

Effective managers should be able to get away from the pack once in a while and close the door. Planning takes private, personal time. Report writing does, too. Sometimes it's good just to lean back, look out the window, and ponder the next move without having to deal with a lot of input.

Good organization planning cuts the reporting ratio down to no more than five or six people reporting to a manager. If the number is five, it's a safe bet that there will be a parade of at least seven into the manager's office, because every organization has its self-appointed, special-privilege people who interpret the boss's open-door policy as a daily invitation to stop and chat. Also, bosses do subvert their own organizations on many occasions by bypassing supervisors to deal directly with workers. Whatever the cause, managers are often subject to interruption and involvement in time-consuming conversations that are personally annoying and/or retard the advancement of work.

As a matter of self-protection, some managers withdraw from the work group, and build fortifications about themselves. While they gain much needed privacy, they lose very important contacts with the work group. Ultimately, such managers find themselves missing important input. They also find themselves giving direction in a very sterile manner. Worst of all, they gain the reputation of being cold, distant, uninterested, and unapproachable.

One very simple way to cut down on office traffic is to hold meetings—the worthwhile, businesslike, project-oriented kind of meetings that actually accomplish 75 percent of the needed interface in a work period. Another way is for the manager to visit the offices and work stations of others. Either or both of these approaches can help in controlling the time required for contacts and eliminating random traffic to a very great extent. Both can erase notions of the boss's coldness, indifference, or superiority.

Isolationism has never worked very well in world affairs, and it's never been effective in industrial matters, either. A people steeped in democratic concepts isn't likely to accept a manager who is seen only on an appointment basis and who doesn't know his way into the back room. Impact managers know that their acceptance as people is the key to their acceptance as directors of work. Rather than shut the world out, they invite it in on an orderly basis.

Lack of Consideration

We earlier discussed the need for a manager's concern about the welfare and progress of those he supervised. In a sense, lack of consideration is an extension of that same idea. It's a very important negative impact item, because it literally tells a subordinate, "I'm important and you're not." It can be demonstrated in innocence and in ignorance, but neither reason is sufficient to excuse it.

When I call a member of our staff and ask, "Have you got a minute? Come on down," the answer is generally, "Be right there." That's because the question and the instruction are given in the same voice, with no pause and no option. When I'm called by my boss, the answer is the same. Yet it's inconceivable that the person called is sitting at his desk just waiting for that call. Managers interrupt ongoing work with not so much as a by-your-leave. It's part of a long-established pattern of business protocol. What seems to excuse it from the stigma of barging in is the fact that telephones don't have eyes. If a manager can't see the person busy at work, he feels he has a right to assume the other person is available.

Lack of consideration is demonstrated more flagrantly by the manager who walks into another's office and takes over. My own work takes me into the offices of other managers to discuss their program needs. There is a purpose in our meeting. Valuable time is represented. Mr. Big walks in, transacts some routine business that might have waited, and generally spends another few minutes on some inconsequential item. When I walk past his office on my way out, he is comfortably seated behind his desk with *The Wall Street Journal.*

I used to work with a manager who had learned that it was rude and counterproductive to walk into another person's office when that person was busy with someone else. So he would look in, disturb the meeting momentarily, return to his own office and call on the telephone. Most of the time, his business was routine and could have waited, but he never thought so.

The manager who interrupts others with the inference that his time is valuable and theirs is not, who demonstrates indifference for the other person's business or personal circumstances, isn't likely to make people want to support his efforts. Conversely, the manager who regularly demonstrates consideration for others finds an understanding and responsive audience whenever he really does find it necessary to inconvenience them.

Some will say that this string of negatives doesn't occur in to-day's business environment. Some will say that they occur and that they're perfectly normal, so why bother? Some may even say that every manager should indulge in some of these negatives from time to time just to show people who's boss. The variety of responses is indicative of the variations in perceptiveness and sensitivity in people. I confess that my own observations tend to center on very good, productive, effective, enduring managers whose impact—up, down, and across the organization—has been achieved by avoiding or minimizing their involvement with these negative characteristics.

Interim Impact Inventory

1. Can you express yourself—even in tight situations—without resorting to harsh, mean, insulting, or unduly demanding words or tones?

2. Do you consider those to whom you give orders and instructions to be reasonable and sensitive human beings?

3. Do you keep your life in a normal balance, avoiding excesses, (even work), so that you pose no unusual problems to yourself or others?

4. Are you capable of keeping your head, controlling your tongue, and maintaining command presence under fire?

5. Are you known as a manager who can resist taking hasty action, especially when there is little time available for planning?

6. Do you attempt to adapt to the corporate environment as much as possible, as opposed to priding yourself on doing your own thing?

7. Can you maintain a warm, friendly in-office relationship with superiors, subordinates, and peers and not let it spill over into private life?

8. Do you build a team atmosphere in which most people have access to most resources and can work easily with other departments and outside contacts?

9. Will you take blame and share credit on just about the same basis at all times?

10. Do you make it a point to treat everyone with reasonable equality, acknowledging merit where it is deserved rather than heaping credit on a favored few?

11. Are you available for consultation on a regular basis—reachable and approachable?

12. Do you show consideration by recognizing the time schedules, the privacy, and the workload of others, reserving interruptions and schedule changes for emergencies?

Part 6
Getting the Most out of Impact by Using It Well

PORTRAIT OF A MANAGER

Unless someone is the sole proprietor of his own business and assumes the management role unchallenged, a manager is selected to do specific things in a particular segment of a business. There is a product to be made or a service to be performed. There is something to take to market and sell. There are records to be kept and reports to be written. Whatever it is, managers are selected to direct and control the work of others who actually do the various jobs involved. In the selection process, therefore, consideration has to be given not only to the individual's ability to understand and perform the work but to his leadership potential as well.

Leadership ability is played out in the many skills, qualities, and attitudes discussed earlier. Together, they make up an ill-defined style of management. In fact, it's safe to say that managers unconsciously adopt a style of management that they're comfortable with or that fits their personality, *hoping* that it will be effective. Will correcting your personality faults or attitudes change your style? Probably. But will the new style achieved be worth the effort?

Before making specific changes in your personal management style, it is wise to take a hard look at some very basic ideas. For instance, what is your view of a manager's work? Also, what is your view of the people currently engaged in the workforce you lead? A look at two of the best observers of modern management may be helpful in putting a perspective on these issues—Douglas McGregor and Frederick Herzberg, whose interesting views are intertwined.

Herzberg posits an analogy between modern man and two biblical figures. He suggests that if we consider modern man's work attitude to be similar to Adam's, that's one thing. If we consider modern man to have the work attitude of Abraham, that's quite another. For a moment, let's refresh our memories about these two personalities.

Genesis tells us that Adam lived at ease in the Garden of Eden. He didn't know anything except that he was to be cared for in comfort. His disobedience of God's admonition not to eat from the tree of knowledge resulted in his banishment from paradise. Part of his punishment was that henceforth he must work. Thus, to Adam, work was what he did because he had to.

Abraham, on the other hand, was challenged to work because he was seen as a responsible, capable human being. God carved out a leadership role for him, and Abraham fulfilled his responsibilities faithfully for many years. He was an achiever who worked not only because the work had to be done but because he saw sense and found satisfaction in doing it.

Herzberg admits there's some of Adam and some of Abraham in all of us. But he emphasizes that it's more satisfying to work toward the accomplishment of goals than to perform mere tasks. He thus encourages managers to provide people with the satisfaction of performing interesting work rather than oblige them to see themselves as toilers who are rewarded with nothing more than the weekly paycheck.

With that in mind, let's look at the McGregor point of view. McGregor suggests that managers tend to see workers in two ways which McGregor classifies as Theory X and Theory Y. This is not necessarily to say that people always fall into these two categories, but that managers tend to perceive them as belonging to one or the other. The Theory X manager sees people as being lazy, not interested in work, in need of prodding, generally security minded, and not much interested in adventure. Conversely, the Theory Y manager sees people as being desirous of work, self-starters, achievers, and much interested in challenges.

Theory X matches the Adam point of view, wherein work is a chore, and Theory Y matches the Abraham point of view, which says work is a challenge. The question is: Which kind of worker do you like to have working for you?

Now own taste points to Theory Y people. When they see work to be done and do it, it means fewer orders to be given. When people like to work and do lots of it, it means fewer missed quotas and less follow-up. When people like to tackle new things or do old jobs in new ways, it means less argument to manage change. If motivation is, as I believe, an inner force released rather than an outer force imposed, I'd like that inner force to be as strong as possible. It seems to me that not only would the work be more interesting, but the management job would be simpler.

But no manager enjoys the efforts of the Theory Y worker if he manages him in a Theory X way. A manager can't operate on a do-this-and-do-that basis and expect people to do much more than they're told. As imperial as directive management may seem—with the king on his throne bidding his servants to follow his every whim—it works only when a manager is willing to stand over workers and see how each step progresses. Workers become what we prejudge them to be.

The worker's point of view: "When he wants something done, he'll tell me. If I don't do it right, he'll tell me. If I do it right, he'll give me another job to do just like the last one. Let him worry about this place; I only work here. What do I do for a living? I work eight hours a day, five days a week, at XYZ Company." Adam was the first Theory X person. God must have adopted a new management style by the time he got to Abraham.

The manager's view of work and his view of the people who are involved in his work group have almost everything to do with how he sees himself and his job. If he sees his own work as a chore, he'll make work a chore for all those involved with him. If he sees his work as stimulating and satisfying beyond hard cash rewards, it is only logical that he would see those who work under his direction as having similar feelings, given the opportunity to have them. If he doesn't particularly like following orders and running errands, should the people in his work group like following orders and running errands? If he likes to have a hand in the design of his workday or the process at which he works, isn't it possible that others might like to have a hand in shaping their work plans, too? How he answers questions like these dictates his management style.

There are some clamped and riveted Theory X managers who would say at this point, "That's all very fine, but it wouldn't work in my organization. I can't trust people to get anything done except if I tell them and keep telling them." I can readily understand the manager who admits to such an attitude. But I would pause to remind him that the reason he can't trust them, that he has to maintain constant control over them, that he has to provide detailed instructions each time he wants something done is the result of his actions, not theirs. His view of himself has caused him to have a similarly rigid view of other people. His view of how he should do his own work results in how they do theirs.

There is nothing wrong with the management posture that says the name of the game is to get the work out. But there is something wrong with the manager who says, "These people are here to help me. Period." The truth of the matter is that he is also there to help them help him. He is there to help them by organizing their work, showing them what has to be done and why, minimizing their concerns, and maximizing their self-confidence. He helps them by cutting them loose to work at objectives instead of tasks. He helps them by encouraging them to be all they're capable of being and proud of what they're doing.

The Theory Y manager also looks at the management role as a get-the-work-out proposition. So he directs his efforts at making his work group aware of the need for achievement and of their part in it. He instructs people on how to do work because he wants them to succeed. He welcomes their initiative and applauds it. He takes advantage of their sense of self-worth and contribution rather than superimposing his own importance on them. He looks for opportunities for the members of his work group for their sake, not just his own. He develops them for responsibility with the assurance that they'll take it.

The kind of manager we're looking for in all this is the manager who doesn't focus his attention on making people feel good so that they'll work for him. He makes people achieve *their* objectives within the framework of the organization's needs. Their own sense of achievement is what makes them feel good. And the better they feel, the harder they work; the harder they work, the more they achieve, ad infinitum.

What does it take to do this? Lay these requirements against the knowledge and skill areas discussed earlier. Lay them against the personal qualities and attitude characteristics discussed earlier. They match. They signal the communicator, the planner, the thoughtful, considerate, vigorous, perceptive, decent human being who can build rapport with others and give them both direction and a sense of worth. This is a manager who knows and expects performance to meet high standards, who is willing to take responsibility and share credit, and do all the other things inherent in good leadership.

It all begins with a point of view which says, in effect, that the manager's role is to make the roles of others effective. It gets the manager's objectives achieved because it gets everyone's objectives achieved. There's nothing phony about it, no manipulation or contrivance. It's not "I win, you lose," but "I win, you win, we win." It's putting all the impact factors into the funnel that feeds into constructive effort *by* everyone and *for* everyone. I've seen it work often enough and well enough to believe in it.

LET THE SYSTEM BE THE SHOWCASE:
IMPACT ON DISPLAY

We began with the hypothesis that the impact manager's effectiveness is measured not only by what he does but by how he does it. Since management involves not only the manager but those who are managed, another premise was offered: Managers function only as people allow them to function. To show the many facets of the manager's impact, a number of observable impact factors were listed and discussed. These ranged all the way from the traditional know-how requirements of a manager to his personal qualities and attitudes—in an admittedly subjective plus-or-minus system of measurements.

To leave it there would be unsatisfying to me. The manager in me compels me to fix things that don't work or make things that do work, work better. The teacher in me prompts the offering of what is to me the one best way to do it. It will come as no surprise, then, that this chapter will deal with a process that has been mentioned here repeatedly: participative management. Further, we'll see how using this management style can develop or enhance the manager's impact.

There's another way to develop a manager's impact—a one-by-one cultivation of each of the impact areas. That's the way Ben Franklin suggested doing it. He contended that anyone could overcome a weakness or develop a strength by concentrating on each item until it was mastered. However, when I look at my own weaknesses and the strengths I'd like to achieve, I have to admit that it would take me a lifetime of concentration to get through them.

With all due reverence to Mr. Franklin, I propose an easier way to develop most of the impact characteristics we've discussed to this point. This is to become committed to the participative management approach and let it systematically provide the required guidance and discipline. More than that, impact is directly proportional to exposure; the manager who uses the participative approach is the manager whose impact is fully on display.

Participative management has been around a long time in one form or another, and it has many adherents. But there are some diehards who argue against it. Before its positive aspects are expressed, we should take a look at some of the negatives and answer them.

Participative management—that's like letting the inmates run the asylum. The very expression of that idea reveals the speaker's attitude toward people in general. If he has that view of workers, there's a long way to go in changing minds. Before a manager can consider the involvement of others in planning and decision making, he has to realize that people can contribute and that such contributions can be meaningful. We're dealing here with a management style that is based on openness and trust; if there isn't any trust to begin with, the program won't work at all.

This is a business, not a democracy. To see participative management as being a democracy (one man, one vote; all in favor say "aye") is a big mistake. Perhaps this is the area of misunderstanding shared by the many managers who shy away from participation by others. Input by people *should* affect a manager's judgment, but he's wrong to let input pass for decision making. It's the manager's expertise that lets him sift the input, come up with the workable elements, guide the thinking of the group into assembling these elements into a workable plan, and get people to do the job. If participative management were pure democracy, I'd quickly invent a new way to manage.

It takes too much time. It does take time. Echoing Parkinson's law, which contends that work expands to fill the time allotted to it, I agree that it's possible to spend too much time in participative sessions. However, it is strictly the prerogative of the manager to call a group session and let it run unrestricted or call a session and terminate it on schedule. That's nothing more than time management, and it's up to the manager to call those shots. On the other hand, think of the time the participative manager saves by preselling those involved on the project to which they've contributed. The explanations of how and why are already done. You spend time at one end while saving it at the other.

It weakens the manager's position. Only if he allows it to do so. Actually, it can strengthen the manager's position, because he then has a splendid forum in which to display his knowledge, judgment, and interest in getting the job done. As he gets to know the participants, they get to know him. His preplanning of a participative session and his handling of it will generally accrue benefits to him.

The manager's position is earned each day, and his positive involvement with people will earn him more support than isolating himself and calling all the shots.

People get confused. The first time, maybe. I recall the first effort I made with a group that had been conditioned to a directive management style. When asked for their suggestions, they were not only reluctant but suspicious. The first session was something less than spectacular and ended in sighs of relief. In a postconference rump session, one of the participants reportedly commented, "This new guy doesn't know very much, does he?" But as the participative approach continued, the contributions made by those involved became more and more productive; the ultimate work yield became a source of pride to all of us.

Participative management bears many labels and is a feature of many disciplines, including management by objectives, organization development, and team building. There are disciples of each, and there are those who insist on full-blown programs. Sprinkled in with all these programs are the thoughts of some eminent behavioral scientists and management experts.

Abraham Maslow's hierarchy of needs is certainly basic to them all. Frederick Herzberg's motivation-hygiene theory, his "satisfiers" and "dissatisfiers," sheds light on the study of workers in organizations. Chris Argyris adds an interesting dimension regarding the integration of individual and organizational objectives. Rensis Likert's concern for the structure of organizations and the interrelationship of the people in them makes an important contribution to the thinking of modern management. And Douglas McGregor's Theory X and Theory Y give tremendous insight into the relationships between workers and managers in the business environment. Managers who wish to improve their understanding of management—their role in relationship to others in the enterprise—should investigate all these theorists.

My reason for mentioning so many schools of thought and the people who contributed to them is simply to confess that my own ideas are borrowed from all. In my opinion, it's not necessary to be a purist or an adherent of any one cult or discipline. It was merely my intention to share a few thoughts about participative management and how a manager can gain impact by employing that style. In my efforts to be brief and practical, I hope I don't appear to be irreverent to these important thinkers.

Participative management is one of three rough alternatives; it sits squarely between directive management and permissive management. At one end of the spectrum, the manager runs the whole show. At the other, he simply lets the show run by itself. Participative management, by whatever name one gives it, could be dubbed a convenient middle-of-the-road management style. This doesn't mean that it's a compromise or a blend of the other two; but it does offer an interesting potential for the manager to slip into either one of the other two styles as circumstances dictate. Although that's not its purpose, any practical manager will see that as a very positive benefit. It bears some explanation.

In most business operations there are pressures that preclude calling meetings or consulting with others. Frequently, something has to be done—right now. There are also some actions that don't require much deliberation, even if time isn't a factor. The manager makes a judgment regarding the matter, calls people in, and tells them what to do and how to do it—directive management. Or the manager is occupied with another project, and an emergency arises; he just has to hope that someone will cope with it satisfactorily—permissive management. My contention is that it's only the participative manager who can slip temporarily into either of these other management styles with any degree of success.

The directive manager certainly is at a loss when he's forced to leave taking action up to someone else. He's even likely to be uneasy when he's on vacation, because he doesn't trust what's happening back at the office. If he has no alternative but to be permissive, he throws his organization into a panic, because the staff has always worked under specific instruction. They're so disciplined that they feel naked without orders. They're strangers to innovation, and they hesitate to act, because they'll probably do the wrong thing.

The permissive manager doesn't slip easily into the directive role, either. In the first place, he isn't comfortable in giving direction, and his work group isn't comfortable in taking it. They're so accustomed to going their own way that they'll probably go that way in the face of instructions to the contrary.

The participative manager can go in either direction. His participative style of management has demonstrated to those involved that he understands them, their work, their problems, and their objectives, and that he is in ultimate control of the organization. They can, perhaps, see some of their own thinking in his thinking as he abruptly changes his approach. If he veers toward the directive style, they accept and respond. If he becomes more permissive, they are preconditioned to accept the responsibility; they already know how the manager might make a decision, because they have been schooled in decision making by him.

Participative management does offer a flexibility that neither of the other two management styles can match. The work group's involvement in previous deliberations concerning what, why, when, and how something should be done makes the members of the group ready to function. They have an appropriate sense of direction, a wholesome sense of discipline, and a healthy sense of self-confidence. What the participative manager has given them in the involvement process is returned in satisfactory action.

Convenience aside, there are also other important benefits of the participative management style. It acknowledges the capabilities of people, and it recognizes their ability to contribute and perform. It moves people considerably up on the Maslow scale, beyond basic human needs and secondary security needs; it takes them into the area of social needs and ego needs, perhaps even into self-actualization. It rewards people, as Herzberg says people want to be rewarded, by being in on things, viewing work as an interesting and fulfilling factor in life. It puts them into McGregor's Theory Y category as people who, given the opportunity, will achieve. It's constructively motivational in every way.

Another obvious benefit of participation is its potential for valuable input. In the privacy of his office, a manager has only a limited view of his operation. Salesmen have a better reading than their manager does of customer resistance to a given product, because they're face to face with customers each day, while he isn't. Foremen have more contact with a manpower problem or a machine difficulty than the superintendent does, because they're out on the plant floor every day. I can manage the development of training programs for my company simply because our instructional staff gives me feedback on what their students need and how it's best to satisfy those needs.

High on the list of benefits from participative management is the fact that people who are involved in problem solving and decision making are considerably better prepared to carry out action. As a result of discussion, they see the rationale of the decision to go in a certain direction, and they see the potential pitfalls of going in another direction. They know why the decision was made and why a certain action has to go a certain way. They also see how their specific role in the activity interfaces with someone else's role. Their improved insight and understanding just has to translate into better performance.

MBO enthusiasts make a long list of advantages that result from a group's involvement in the setting of objectives. For instance, when people are involved in setting objectives, they tend to set higher goals for themselves than when goals are set for them. Sales managers who have tried this support the claim; their salesmen set higher quotas for themselves than the boss does, and they don't complain about having to fill them. Furthermore, those who have had a hand in setting their own goals work harder to achieve them than when they are simply handed them. It's a case of motivation going in and motivation coming out.

Despite the fact that we perceive work groups as groups, they are made up of individuals who often work alone or in smaller groups. They often don't see the effect of total group effort. They often aren't aware of what contribution is being made by another person or group of people within the organization. Thus, the participative process is a communication system that keeps people informed and interested. And there is improved credibility when workers can get information from others in the group, not just from the manager.

Are there any limitations to or inconveniences in the participative style? I think there are, but they needn't stop a manager from trying it. It seems to me that workers expect some management decisions to be made exclusively by management. Some informal opinion sampling might be done, but no more than that. People don't expect to be consulted on everything; indeed, it would be a waste of time. I'm sure participation can yield the greatest benefits with the least awkwardness when it's confined to small, related groups, that is, the top executive with key department managers, department managers with their subordinate managers, the plant superintendent with general foremen, the general foremen with their foremen, and the foremen with their work groups.

There is in this Likert's linking-pin effect, in which the superior in one group is a subordinate in the next higher one. Ultimately, the feedback from the sweeper on the third shift does get to the president of the company. The advantage of a smaller group is the ability of each manager to pay close attention to the contributions made by each member of the group. In addition, the groups begin to identify themselves as groups; since they work as groups, such identification is doubly advantageous.

But do people on the end of the line really want to participate? Isn't there a limit on how far down in an organization the participative process goes? Obviously, some managements think so, because they believe in the involvement of a select high-level group and no more. Yet there is evidence that people at all levels of work are interested in expression. The very existence of unions, in my opinion, is as much for the expression of the guy on the line about ordinary matters as it is for the redress of grievances. Suggestion plans are a well-accepted, formalized type of participation; wherever they are well administered, people take part.

Can a participative style be carried out in a directive company? It stands to reason that, the more general the style, the greater its acceptance and the more fruitful its use. But if a manager is willing to try it, it can be made to work. At Chrysler, a strong movement is under way to encourage use of the organization development concept because top management sees value in it; yet not all departments use it. Conversely, some departments have used participative management approaches for years without the formality of top-level support. It comes down to how the individual manager feels and how he communicates with his workers.

Here are some hints on how to employ any system of participative management:

1. Begin with the idea that you are working with Theory Y people. Only with such an attitude can the program work.

2. Begin with a real problem. This style of management isn't just an exercise in group process. Make it a reasonably small problem, if you will, but not one with simple answers or only one point of view.

3. Get the right people there. Mind the politics and the balance of the group. Be sure that those who participate can make a real contribution to thought processes and that parts of the work which arise out of the process can be assigned directly to the participants.

4. Prethink the problem, but expect solutions that may be different from yours. Going into a participative session with all the

answers can result in a management-by-endorsement meeting.

5. Present the problem carefully. Eliminate as much bias as possible in the facts presented. Leave the way open for good questions and a free exchange of ideas.

6. Establish the purpose of the discussion and the parameters of action. Tell participants that their suggestions are encouraged and that, when taken together, these suggestions will bear on the ultimate decision. Make it clear that no one contribution is more important than any other, and that in the end the decision may favor a minority opinion rather than a majority one.

7. Make some decisions on the spot and delay others, as circumstances dictate. The function of the group is to contribute, not to decide.

8. Reveal decisions to the group as soon as possible. If further explanation is necessary, explain further. The participative process aims at enlisting cooperation, not destroying it.

9. Thank contributors for their input. Where possible, isolate key contributions for special recognition.

10. Make assignments that will fully implement the decision. Attempt to balance work wherever possible.

11. Follow up to be sure work is progressing properly. Provide interim reports at subsequent meetings. Have people assigned tell what *they* are doing.

12. Report complete progress as early as is convenient. Each time an achievement is noted, it paves the way for further achievement.

The above listing oversimplifies the participative procedure, but it shows the many opportunities the manager has to develop and display impact characteristics.

Without dominating the participative procedure, the manager has a splendid opportunity to demonstrate his knowledge and skill. The manager's insights are revealed by the questions he asks, the comments he makes, the contributions he acknowledges, and the conclusions he reaches. Then, as he organizes the work and apportions it, he demonstrates his ability to plan. All this is done with communications skills that speak for themselves. In short, if the manager has it, people will come to see it—first hand!

The manager's personal qualities and his attitude can be well displayed in the participative area. How better than in an informal, business-oriented atmosphere can he project his image to others in the company? Throughout the procedure, however, the manager has to be sure that the impact factors he's revealing are the positive ones, not the negatives!

Whether the manager is the superior, conducting business with a subordinate, or a subordinate contributing in the presence of peers and superiors, he is still in the arena to see and hear—to be seen and heard—by others. There's no escaping the exposure, but there's no other arena that gives it so well.

Let's go back to Ben Franklin for a moment. If the manager evaluates himself and comes up short, perhaps he should take the old Doctor's advice and solve a few of those negatives or crank up a few of those positives before taking them into the forum.

A closing note: Managers *are* judged by what they do. But how they do it is vitally important. Managers are chosen to direct the enterprise, but those who are directed also have a great deal to say about it. The manager who ignores this concept is missing an important angle on the management role.

A brilliant philosopher named W. MacNiele Dixon said it well: "It is not the sails but the unseen wind that moves the ship."

There may not seem to be much room for philosophy in the business office, but it is a good idea for all managers to paste that idea in their hats. To the extent they understand and manage their operations with such understanding, they can manage with impact and success!

A Postscript

Some well-accepted steps in the learning process are recognition of knowledge, assimilation of knowledge, application of knowledge, and generation of new knowledge. We use each of these steps as we first learn and continue to learn management skills.

The first two steps—recognition and assimilation—show how important it is to learn from others. A portion of it can come from textbooks, but more of it comes from association with top-flight managers. I've been fortunate in having had the opportunity to work under and be around some very good ones. They built their impact scores in different ways, yet each had certain strengths in common.

Every outstanding manager I have ever known began with an exceptional knowledge of the particular part of the business he was responsible for. Because this was true, each had a solid base of self-confidence. Further, each was so secure within himself that he was open to input—research, opinion, innovative ideas—without feeling any threat to his position. My favorite managers were people who expressed themselves freely and expected others to do so as well. They established rapport within the work group and beyond it. Their political adeptness was wholesome, not contrived. They were good communicators, not because they turned a clever phrase, but because they were clear and logical and had the capacity to sell their points of view.

As far as I know, they never took a course in or read a book on participative management, yet they practiced it. They took advantage—in the best sense of the term—of the people who surrounded them. Seldom did I receive an assignment from any of them before I had already accepted the task. They were more friend and counselor than boss. They knew how to harness creativity and get it on track with clear objective setting. Each, in his own way, had a talent for organizing a project, getting the right people at the right task, and balancing the workload. They knew when to step in and when to get out of the way. They knew how to set up challenges without making a subordinate feel driven to the wall. They got cooperation because they generated a cooperative climate and set their own example of it.

There are three, in particular, I would cite as exemplary in the impact characteristics discussed here. The circumstances were widely separated—different kinds of work, different companies and environments, and different times. Yet all had the impact factors delineated above: Ab Martin of the General Electric Company, Marv Lindeman of Lindeman Advertising, and Mario Garbin of Chrysler Corporation. They should have had the pleasure of meeting one another!

A fourth with whom I never worked but with whom I spent hundreds of hours in serious conversation was Alex Lumsden, my uncle. He landed in this country from his native Scotland with five dollars in his pocket, and worked himself up to head a three-plant steel company—Ajax Steel of Detroit. A blacksmith by trade, he worked in rough surroundings in the days when management always called all the shots. He became head of the River Rouge steel complex of the Ford Motor Company before he struck out on his own, and he saw management move from the tough to the thoughtful, from coercion to leadership, from strength to sophistication, and from tasks to objectives. He believed strongly in two things that marked him as a leader: the dignity of work and the primacy of the person. He prospered with these and other impact characteristics. So did those with whom he was associated.

There are others as well from whom I have learned a lot about management. Some were very good managers and some were pretty awful. Not to name them will, I hope, do no disservice to any of them—on either side of the aisle. I thank these managers, wherever they stand on the impact scale, because they demonstrated the additive and subtractive power of each item on it.

Finally, I learned from myself about the application of knowledge and the generation of new knowledge. The writing of this book has made me see myself more clearly in my own management role. The words are behind me, but the job of raising my impact score is still ahead.

I feel obliged to try.

Index